Personal
Spiritual Warfare

Written by
Betty Miller-Haddix

Personal Spiritual Warfare

First Edition Published 1991
Revised Version 2014
Digital & Paperback Publishing 2025

Printed and bound in the United States of America

ISBN 978-1-57149-018-6

CHRIST UNLIMITED PUBLISHING
P.O. Box 850
Dewey, Arizona 86327
All Rights Reserved
Printed in U.S.A.

www.BibleResources.org

Scripture quotations are taken from the King James Version (KJV) unless otherwise indicated.

TABLE OF CONTENTS

PREFACE

When we mention "Spiritual Warfare," many Christians do not even know that there is a war going on. The church has not yet dealt with the powers of darkness as an enlightened and united "Body of Christ." However, in the last few years, certain individuals have been raised up by God to share significant revelation on spiritual warfare. Betty is one of those warriors to whom God has given the message on how to get victory in your life through spiritual warfare.

This book exposes the devices of Satan and will give you the knowledge of how to overcome the devil in his personal attacks on you and your family.

As a pastor for many years, I have dealt with people who had severe problems with their personal finances, marriage, rebellious children, fear, anger, etc. I came to the realization that each child of God must put on the armor of God and do battle in the spirit to see victory in their personal lives.

The principles in this book have been proven valid because they are based on the Word of God. They have been practiced in our local church with victorious lives as the result. May you have the same results as you read and apply the principles in this timely book.

Yours in His Service,

Pastor Bud Miller
June 1991

Note: Pastor R.S. "Bud" Miller went to be with the Lord on March 18, 2020. Betty Miller has since remarried in the fall of 2023 and her name is now Betty Miller-Haddix and her new husband is Earl Haddix. They serve the Lord together, as His servants, to maintain the BibleResources.org website and are the leaders and directors of Christ Unlimited Ministries. The ministry headquarters are in Dewey, Arizona, USA.

FOREWORD

The Lord is giving many in the Body of Christ new revelation teaching about "spiritual warfare" and this book is an instruction manual for you to navigate successfully through the warzone. It is needed at this time and is given for our understanding of this practice. It deals with how to be effective in "spiritual warfare" by first obtaining the victories in your own personal lives.

Personal "spiritual warfare" must precede taking a larger territory for God. If we have not obtained victory in our personal lives, in our finances, in our marriage and other relationships, in overcoming the emotional pressures of fear, anger, hurt, etc., then how are we ever going to deal with the principalities over our cities and territories?

This book will show you how to obtain your personal victories. It is one of the few books that I have written in which I share much of my own personal battles with the enemy. Through obedience to God's Word and His guidance, we can overcome all the onslaughts of the devil. May this book help you in your own *personal spiritual warfare*.

One of His Warriors,
Betty Miller-Haddix

NOTE: In the age of "AI" (Artificial Intelligence), when so many people are using it to generate the writing of their books; I thought I should make a statement regarding the writing of this book: I <u>did</u> <u>not</u> use "AI" to generate this book, nor was a ghost writer involved. I used "IA" (the great "I AM"). I wrote this book myself, at the leading of the Holy Spirit and under His anointing. I did have help with editing and am grateful for all who assisted in that process. I pray you are blessed with revelation as you read.

DEDICATION

I would especially like to dedicate this book to all the intercessory prayer warriors who have stood with me over the years. Their prayers made it possible for me to experience many of my own personal spiritual victories.

Intercessors are the unseen heroes in any ministry. The Lord has large crowns for each of you. I wrote this book in 1991, as Bud and I pastored a local church in Dewey, Arizona. We were teaching our flock how to overcome and we also taught these principles in our Bible School at the time. However, these same principles are just as timely today as when I first penned them.

Earl Haddix, my new husband, has technical skills, along with many other amazing talents. His gift of understanding and applying the necessary technology applications to the manuscripts made it possible to digitize this book and the other end time book I wrote, *"Mark of God or Mark of the Beast."* Both books were written and published in the same year. Now these books will be available in digitized versions at the **BibleResources.org** website.

May the Lord strengthen you and give you His revelation as you read and apply the truths in this book so you may also be one of His servants and warriors! May His kingdom come and His will be done in the earth as it is in heaven!

Blessings,
Betty Miller-Haddix
June 2025

INTRODUCTION

Most Christians agree that we are living in the last days of the end times. Jesus himself spoke to us in **Matthew 24:6, "And ye shall hear of wars and rumors of wars …"** and **verse seven** says, **"For nation shall rise against nation, and kingdom against kingdom …"** In the natural realm wars are taking place, but also there is a spiritual war that is raging in God's Kingdom, as the saints of God are doing battle against Satan's kingdom. Today many are calling "good" "evil" and "evil" "good." **(Isaiah 5:20: "Woe unto them that call evil good, and good evil; that put darkness for light, and light for darkness; that put bitter for sweet, and sweet for bitter!")** We must know what the Bible says about how to overcome any evil attacks against us personally.

We are admonished in **Ephesians 6:10-18** to put on the armor of God and do battle in the spirit realm by using our weapons outlined in these verses. The book cover image portrays these scriptures. This book is written especially for those entering the battle on a personal level. Before we begin to take larger territory, we must accomplish victory in our own lives, our families and our churches.

This book exposes the devices of Satan, giving God's saints the knowledge of how to overcome the devil, who tries to destroy Christians in their personal lives. This is the hour for the church to rise up and overcome Satan's onslaught of sickness, depression, lack, fear and poverty and all temptation in our personal lives. We can then come together corporately and use our weapons of prayer and praise to take greater territory in our nations for God.

His grateful servant,

Betty Miller-Haddix

PERSONAL SPIRITUAL WARFARE

Chapter 1
Recognizing the Enemy in Personal Warfare

Spiritual Discernment

Spiritual warfare has become a subject much discussed and preached among Christians today. At this present hour, Holy Spirit is emphasizing this subject to the church.

Warfare means "waging an assault" against an enemy. God and His people are at war against Satan and demon powers. Since this warfare is in the invisible spiritual realm, it is called *"spiritual warfare."* We must understand the spiritual realm and be able to recognize the enemy and his tactics if we are to obtain victory.

The place to begin our warfare is on a personal level. Unless we are victorious.in our personal lives, we will never be able to help others gain their needed victories, much less be able to battle spiritually for our cities and nation. We must learn to rule and reign in our individual lives by casting down the flesh or carnal desires and yielding to Christ in all things. To win our spiritual battles, we must be aggressive against our enemy, Satan. We cannot be passive. We must take the initiative. Our position must be the <u>offensive</u> one, rather than a <u>defensive</u> one. Truly, God is calling us, His people, to rise up and war against our common enemy.

We are in a war. Note how the Bible describes our warfare: **"For though we walk in the flesh, we do not war after the flesh: (For the weapons of our warfare are not carnal, but mighty through God to the pulling down of strongholds;) Casting down imaginations, and every high thing that exalteth itself against the knowledge of God, and bringing into captivity every thought to the** obedience of Christ; And having in a readiness to revenge all disobedience, when your obedience is fulfilled" (2 Corinthians 10:3-6).

This passage points out that our warfare is in the spiritual realm, and then asks, **"Do ye look on things after the outward appearance?" (2 Corinthians 10:7a).**

That is a good question: Are we looking at things after the outward appearance? If so, we are missing the reality that we live in a spiritual realm with an ongoing battle in that realm. We cannot rely upon the appearance of things in the natural world because it is the spirit realm that is influencing the natural realm. Thus, even though we are flesh and blood, we are not to walk after the flesh, but rather after the spirit. **"That the righteousness of the law might be fulfilled in us, who walk not after the flesh, but after the Spirit" (Romans 8:4).**

God wants His people to see with the eyes of the spirit and not look after the outward appearance. If we walk close to Him, being totally yielded, He will give us discernment to see into the spirit realm. Then we can truly understand what is going on.

Looking at things with the natural eye will never suffice. **"But as it is written, Eye hath not seen, nor ear heard, neither have entered into the heart of man, the things which God hath prepared for them that love him. But God hath revealed them unto us by his Spirit: for the Spirit searcheth all things, yea, the deep things of God. For what man knoweth the things of a man, save the spirit of man which is in him? even so the things of God knoweth no man, but the Spirit of God. Now we have received, not the spirit of the world, but the spirit which is of God; that we might know the things that are freely** given to us of God. Which things also we speak, not in the words which man's wisdom teacheth, but which the Holy Ghost teacheth; comparing spiritual things with spiritual. But the natural man receiveth not the things of the Spirit of God: for they are foolishness unto him: neither can he know them, because they are spiritually discerned" (1 Corinthians 2:9-14).

Spiritual discernment is crucial. As God gives us spiritual eyes, we will see things correctly. For example, in the church, we will see one another in the proper light as brothers and sisters in Christ. Instead of focusing on one another's faults and shortcomings, we will be set to help each other overcome any weaknesses. We will help through supportive prayers and by showing love and kindness to one another.

Spiritual discernment will open our awareness of the spirit realm. What is the spirit realm? It is a realm made up of two kingdoms, one of darkness and one of light. While God rules the kingdom of light, Satan is master over the kingdom of darkness.

Fallen Angels
This evil master over the kingdom of darkness is our enemy. In any war, it is essential to identify the enemy. Satan started out as a good angel. God created him as a perfect angel. Originally named Lucifer (light bearer), he was the archangel in charge of praise and worship. As music director, he led the angels in their worship before the throne of God. The Bible describes him as the *"anointed cherub"* having *"tabrets"* (small drums) in him. Descriptions of Satan can be found in **Ezekiel 28** and **Isaiah 14**. Much of the world's music today has become increasingly perverted and depraved. Satan, who once oversaw that realm in

heaven, and then upon losing it, has tried to gain influence again, by corrupting music and praise in the earth realm.

What happened to Lucifer? How did he become Satan, an adversary? Lucifer changed from good to evil when pride entered him. He boasted, **"... I will exalt my throne above the stars of God ... I will be like the most High" (Isaiah 14:13b,14b).** When he decided to exalt himself above God, iniquity was found in him **(Ezekiel 28:15).** At that point, Lucifer became Satan. He was cast down to the earth, and in his fall, he took with him a third of the angels who were also in rebellion **(Revelation 12:4,9).** These fallen angels are now evil invisible spirits that, along with Satan, harass and torment the people of God. They are all part of the spiritual kingdom of darkness.

Good Angels

Satan's kingdom of darkness is, of course, totally opposite to God's kingdom of light. In God's kingdom, the angels are good. They are invisible servants that help God's people. **"Are they not all ministering spirits, sent forth to minister for them who shall be heirs of salvation?" (Hebrews 1:14).** Even though we do not see them, the angels are ever present to help and protect us. These are referred to as our "guardian angels."

These angels love to be around when we praise and worship God. As we enter into praise and worship, angels come on the scene eager to join in. That is why many battles are won simply by singing praises to God. The presence of the angels who have come to join the praise drives away Satan's evil spirits. Note in **2 Chronicles 20:15-22** that the moment the Israelites **"... began to sing and to praise ..." (v. 22a),** they gained the victory over their enemies. God sometimes allows us to see angels, or they can be sent to us with a message. However, we must discern and confirm they are

4

good angels and not false or fallen angels as the devil and his demons can impersonate good angels.

2 Corinthians 11:14 "And no marvel; for Satan himself is transformed into an angel of light."

Another instance of evil angels fleeing was when David played his harp for King Saul who was tormented by demons; the sound of the music caused the demons to flee in **1 Samuel 16:14-23:**

14 But the Spirit of the LORD departed from Saul, and an evil spirit from the LORD troubled him.

15 And Saul's servants said unto him, Behold now, an evil spirit from God troubleth thee.

16 Let our lord now command thy servants, which are before thee, to seek out a man, who is a cunning player on an harp: and it shall come to pass, when the evil spirit from God is upon thee, that he shall play with his hand, and thou shalt be well.

17 And Saul said unto his servants, Provide me now a man that can play well, and bring him to me.

18 Then answered one of the servants, and said, Behold, I have seen a son of Jesse the Beth-lehemite, that is cunning in playing, and a mighty valiant man, and a man of war, and prudent in matters, and a comely person, and the LORD is with him.

19 Wherefore Saul sent messengers unto Jesse, and said, Send me David thy son, which is with the sheep.

20 And Jesse took an ass laden with bread, and a bottle of wine, and a kid, and sent them by David his son unto Saul.

21 And David came to Saul, and stood before him: and he loved him greatly; and he became his armourbearer.

22 And Saul sent to Jesse, saying, Let David, I pray thee, stand before me; for he hath found favour in my sight.

23 And it came to pass, when the evil spirit from God was upon Saul, that David took an harp, and played with his hand: so Saul was refreshed, and was well, and the evil spirit departed from him.

Though the angels are assigned to help us, we cannot directly command their assistance. Note Jesus' words: **"Thinkest thou that I cannot now pray to my Father, and he shall presently give me more than twelve legions of angels?" (Matthew 26:53).** Jesus Himself did not command the angels; He said the Father could send them. No Scripture supports the idea that we can directly command good angels.

Indirectly, however, we can influence their activity. As we pray to the Father, He may send us angelic assistance. Their assistance is in response to our prayers, but it is directed by God's command, not ours. Particularly in the Old Testament, many times there is only a mention of angels involved in certain things and the Bible does not distinguish as to if they are good or evil angels. We must determine if an angel is good or evil by what they are doing. If it is evil work then they would be bad angels; however, if they were helping people by good works then these angels would be good angels.

Angelic Domains

We are not given authority to command the good angels anywhere in the Bible. However, the fallen angels are subject to the authority of the Holy Spirit within us. These demons (evil angels) must submit as we use the name of Jesus, and that name alone. Jesus said, **"… In my name shall they cast out devils …" (Mark 16:17b).** In Jesus' name, we have the authority to command demons to leave.

While there are myriads of angels, the Bible names only three: *Lucifer* (now Satan), *Gabriel*, and *Michael*. These three are named because they are archangels originally placed over different areas of God's kingdom. As already mentioned, Lucifer was the music director in charge of praise and worship (**Ezekiel 28:13-14**). Gabriel has been placed over communication; He is the messenger angel (**Luke 1:19**). And Michael is the warrior angel, responsible for guarding heaven (**Revelation 12:7**).

When we are in spiritual warfare, Michael is on our side. Note **Daniel 10**: As Daniel was fasting and praying, the prince of Persia (an evil angel) battled against him, determined to keep the Word of the Lord from reaching him. It was only when Michael entered the warfare that the answer came through. An angel told Daniel that his prayers had been heard from the first day; but there was warfare in heaven that had delayed the answer for 21 days (**Daniel 10:12-13**).

That is spiritual warfare. It is the same today as it was in Daniel's day. God hears our prayers the moment we pray, but sometimes there is a battle in the spirit realm holding back that answer. We must stand in faith as we enter into spiritual warfare until the answer to our prayer is manifested in the natural realm. God will send His angels to assist us as we continue to pray and stand in faith.

Satan's Influence Over People

Our warfare is not **"... after the flesh" (2 Corinthians 10:3).** So often, we mistakenly think our battle is with other human beings. That is not true. Our battle is not with a spouse, a boss, or a neighbor or a relative or whomever might seem to be a source of harassment. Instead, our battle is with Satan and his demonic powers. Of course, many times people come under Satan's influence and harass us. If we use our authority in Christ, we can free people from that satanic influence. We can bind the demons that are influencing them and loose the Holy Spirit to move upon their hearts.

For example, we may know someone who believes a lie of the devil. A spirit of error may have him totally deluded. Because this person is under spiritual deception, he may even be speaking against the truth. What can we do? Should we respond in the flesh and launch into an intense argument? Of course not! We simply war in the spirit. We use the name of Jesus and take authority over the spirit of error that is deceiving him. After all, it is the enemy that blinds the minds of men. **"In whom the god of this world hath blinded the minds of them which believe not, lest the light of the glorious gospel of Christ, who is the image of God, should shine unto them" (2 Corinthians 4:4).**

We should pray that these deceived ones see the light of God's truth. If they can see the light concerning Christ, and if they can understand the love and goodness of God, they will want to follow Him rather than the devil. They are heading in the wrong direction because the enemy has blinded them. Our prayers can push back the powers of darkness and release the truth of the Holy Spirit to their hearts. As they begin to see the truth, they will usually choose the light. After all, a person would have to be insane to knowingly pick hell over heaven once they saw the difference. Once people are free from deceiving spiritual influences, most will choose good rather than evil. Of course, there are some who are incorrigible. However, we are still called to pray for them and that releases the Lord to deal with them as He knows best, since He knows all hearts. Through our prayers, people will respond to the Holy Spirit. This is one thing spiritual warfare does. It pushes back the powers of darkness so that people can hear the Holy Spirit and be influenced by Him.

Certainly, this does not suggest we have power over another person's will. We have power over demons influencing a person, but not over the will of that person. Everyone has free will. That is how God has created us, as moral beings with free choice. Our freedom to choose includes the choice of where we will spend eternity - in heaven or in hell.

When a man chooses hell rather than heaven, he is going against God's will. God is **"… not willing that any should perish …" (2 Peter 3:9b).** For that matter, hell was not created for man. It was **"… prepared for the devil and his angels" (Matthew 25:41b).** However, because man has a free will, he can choose to go there, even though it is not God's will.

Three Strategies of the Devil

Satan, on the other hand, wants to fill hell with as many souls as possible. He wants men in hell, and he wants their stay on earth to be hellish. To this end, he uses these three things against men: *ignorance of the Word of God (the Bible), deception* and *rebellion.*

What happens when a man is ignorant of the Word of God? He will not know the ways of God. Ignorance of God's ways leads to destruction. **"My people are destroyed for lack of knowledge …" (Hosea 4:6a).** Likewise, deception leads to destruction. Satan causes people to believe his lies, even sending out false representatives of Christ. **"For many shall come in my name, saying, I am Christ; and shall deceive many" (Matthew 24:5).** Under deception, men follow Satan, rather than God. Rebellion, also, leads to destruction as it causes men's hearts to turn away from God. **"… a stubborn and rebellious generation; a generation that set not their heart aright, and whose spirit was not stedfast with God" (Psalm 78:8b).** Ignorance of the Word of God, deception, and rebellion—all three of these will lead to destruction.

Self-Examination Before Warfare

Since we have a foe that is out to destroy us, we must continually be on guard. If we find ourselves in conflict with someone, the ultimate cause of that dissension is Satan. Therefore, we need to battle his forces, not other people. In our battle, we must first fully submit ourselves to the will of God and make sure we are not being influenced by demonic powers. We could be the ones in the wrong.

Thus, our prayer could be along these lines: *"Lord, You know I am having a problem with that brother. I believe his actions are not of You. But is there something in my heart causing this strife? What is in me that needs to be dealt with? Is the enemy influencing me? Have I done anything, or failed to do something that has created this problem?"*

Let us examine our own hearts first whenever we run into problems. We are to first submit unto God and then resist the devil. **James 4:7 says, "Submit yourselves therefore to God. Resist the devil, and he will flee from you."** Notice, this verse says the devil "will flee" **not** "maybe he will flee."

As we first check our own hearts and make any necessary corrections, we may find that the problems clear up, but not always. We may still have some praying to do against demonic influences. And when those demons are working through another individual it can be difficult to discern the person from the demons.

Our tendency is to lump the person together with the demons. We often do not want anything to do with a person under demonic influence or control, since our natural response is to stay away from demons. We do not want to be around demonic assault, whether it is in the form of strife, anger, hatred, bitterness or however it manifests itself. We are repelled by evil spirits, so we want to get rid of the person under demonic influence. But that is the wrong response. Instead, we should forgive and love the person, all the while praying against any evil spirits influencing him.

It is not easy to love the person harassing us. But we are commanded to **"... Love your enemies, bless them that curse you, do good to them that hate you, and pray for them which despitefully use you, and persecute you" (Matthew 5:44b).** We cannot fulfill this in our own strength. We will need to pray, *"Lord, give me Your love for this person because I am not able to love them."* And God will do it; He will enable us to love our enemies.

A dramatic example of this occurred in the life of the late Corrie Ten Boom. During World War II, Corrie was imprisoned for hiding Jews in her Dutch home, even though she was not Jewish herself. She and other family members suffered terribly while imprisoned, with only Corrie surviving the ordeal. Despite the abuse she suffered, Corrie prayed for her guards and set her heart to minister God's love to them. She was determined to overcome evil with good. **"Be not overcome of evil, but overcome evil with good"**

(Romans 12:21). Corrie realized that the real enemy was Satan, not the Nazi guards. Years later after the war, she saw fruit from her prayers. One of the guards, after receiving salvation through Christ, came to Corrie and asked her forgiveness. Such is the power of prayer.

All Sin Invites Satan's Attacks

Prayer accomplishes so much; yet most of us pray so little. As a result, we end up with many problems that we would otherwise not have. Prayerlessness opens wide the door for demonic powers to strike us, as Satan takes advantage of our passivity. Christians may cry out, *"Why are all these terrible things happening to me? I have not done anything!"* That is the problem, we have not done *anything*! We have been passive. We have not done our spiritual homework; we have not been in prayer. We have neglected to do the things that need be done to hold back the enemy. **"Therefore to him that knoweth to do good, and doeth it not, to him it is sin" (James 4:17).** Remember our sin invites the enemy into our lives. It may not be a "sin of commission," (committing a sin) but rather a "sin of omission" that opens the door for the devil to attack us. We "omit" doing something we should have done.

This means it is counted as a sin to omit doing something we should be doing. We usually think of sin being something we did wrong, but it can also be something we failed to do. Disobedience falls in this category. If God tells us to do something and we disobey, then that is sin as well. God does not automatically prevent Satan from attacking us. Instead, our immunity comes as we line up with scriptural principles that deter Satan. Christians who are ignorant of these principles often suffer needlessly at the hand of their enemy. It is not that they have deliberately sinned; it is simply that they lack wearing the whole armor of God. God does not restrain the devil unless we do the things that cause Satan's restraint. Many precious Christians are being walked on by the devil simply because they do not know what to do, or how to deal with the enemy.

God will give us immunity from Satan if we apply His biblical principles to our lives. One essential principle requires that we root out any sins that might beset us. If there are areas of sin or spiritual weakness in our lives, demonic powers can attach themselves to those weak spots. For example, a man may have a quick temper. If he has not dealt with that temper by bringing it to the cross to be crucified; if he has not cried out to God until deliverance comes, then a "spirit of anger" will be attracted to his own individual anger. That evil spirit, in a hidden way, can attach itself to the man's temper. Once there, the evil spirit will masquerade itself so that observers cannot separate the man's anger from the "spirit of anger." As the demon comes forth, the man loses control over it.

In the beginning, he might have been able to control himself, but no longer. What had previously been a flesh problem with a quick temper has now become a spiritual problem requiring deliverance. Unless a Spirit-filled Christian can discern the presence of that demon and cast it out, the oppressed man may be plagued by anger all his life. Alone, the man is powerless against the demon because the only power that can bring deliverance is God's power.

As a person continues sinning, they open themselves up to demonic oppression and possession. At that point, saying "no" to the sin becomes nearly impossible. That is why the wonderful idea, "Just say 'no' to drugs," will not work for those with a demon of addiction. Such addicts are driven by demonic powers to the extreme of even killing others for drugs. They need deliverance so they can be free to say "no."

The time to say "no" is when *first* faced with temptation. Saying "no" to temptation may work at the beginning. Anyone can say "no" when first tempted because at that point he does not have a demon inside driving him to sin. The demon is outside of the person. Upon being tempted, the person needs to resist and come against the temptation by the Word of God. If he decides to continually embrace the sin, a demon can enter in and deliverance will become necessary, as they are now being controlled by a demon.

Most of societies' rehabilitation centers for substance abusers fall short at this point because they do not deal with the need for spiritual deliverance. True, there is physical addiction, but the greater problem is the evil spirit driving an addict to crave the very thing that could destroy him.

Years ago, I was addicted to nicotine. I began smoking as a teenager; foolishly thinking it was the adult thing to do. My first cigarette caused me to cough and feel so dizzy and nauseated that I had to lie down. Our bodies are designed to reject harmful substances, but the will is stronger than our natural defenses, so eventually the body adjusts to the poison.

As I kept forcing myself to smoke, my body accepted it. When a person first begins to sin in an area, he does it by his will without demonic compulsion. But as he continually yields to the temptation, an evil spirit can enter the picture; the demon will have him hooked. He may claim, "I can lay down this sin any time I want to." In the initial stages of his sin, that may be true. But once he is under demonic compulsion, he cannot permanently be free from his sin without divine help in the form of deliverance.

Divine help includes deliverance through the actual casting out of demons. A demon can be cast out or it can be "starved out." Some people, through a strong battle of their wills, *"starve out"* the demon. They resist the sin long enough that the demon no longer has anything to feed on.

Sin is Progressive

All sin is progressive. Note the following adage: *"The man takes a drink; then the drink takes a drink; then the drink takes the man."* As we fall deeper and deeper into sin, demons attach themselves to us, bringing us into bondage. An example of this can be seen in the life of one of Uganda's former rulers, Idi Amin.

When my husband and I went on a mission trip to Uganda shortly after Amin's expulsion, we witnessed the horrifying after-effects of his demonic rule. He committed the most torturous atrocities imaginable. He was so demon-possessed that he cut off his own best friend's head, whom he felt had betrayed him, and put it under refrigeration so he could look at it every day. This ruler ravaged all of Uganda. Wondering how he ended up so depraved, I heard the Lord speak to my heart, *"He started out like everyone else; just an innocent baby born into the world. He became so depraved because sin is progressive."* Sometimes it is our own sin, sometimes it is the sins of our parents that lead us to progressively sin.

If we do not root out sin in our lives now, we could end up like Idi Amin. That may seem improbable, but sin rapidly grows; it invites increasingly more sin. A little deception invites more deception, and it keeps growing. That is why God is calling His church to be cleansed. He wants His people hungering and thirsting for righteousness and holiness, no longer embracing sin.

Victory Over Sin

On the positive side, righteousness is also progressive. As we press into God and obey His Word, righteousness grows within us. The more we press in and the closer we draw to Him, the more we obey, the more we absorb His Word, the more His holy character is formed within us! We become like His Son, as the character of Christ does an ongoing work within us.

On the other hand, if we follow our flesh and do what Satan wants, we will take on his evil character. Seeing our weak areas as an open door into our lives, Satan will harass us with his evil spirits. Thus, we cannot afford even one hidden pet sin. If we hang on to that one sin, the enemy will work through that area to destroy us, even if he must wait 20 years to time his attack. Let us cry out, *"O God, cleanse me from all sin. Make me holy and pure like You."* Christ Himself exhorted us, **"Be ye therefore perfect, even as your Father which is in heaven is perfect" (Matthew 5:48).** Holiness is what God wants.

Some people will use the feeble excuse, *"The devil made me do it."* Granted, our battle is against Satan and his wicked hordes, not against flesh and blood. However, man is without excuse. There are wicked men with wicked hearts because they have chosen to do evil and thereby have allowed demonic powers to enter in. When the temptation first came, they yielded to it; and as they came under demonic bondage in that weak area, demons compelled them to continually repeat their sin. Does this mean we become powerless against the enemy? By no means! As Christians we have authority over our foe. A victory in the life of Smith Wigglesworth shows this. Wigglesworth, known as the "apostle of faith," was used by God to heal many people and even raise the dead. However, he was plagued by a bad temper. Determined to change, he set aside prayer time and cried out, *"God, I cannot go any farther with this thing in my life; deliver me!"* He sought God until, ten prayer-filled days later, he finally broke free.

The reason most of us do not break free is we do not genuinely want to. We want to hang on to our sin. If we sincerely desire deliverance, God can set us free. But we have to get serious enough. Are we willing to fast and pray? Are we humble enough to ask others to pray with us? Are we willing to do whatever it takes? Of course, our battle for freedom may take time, especially if the sin we have embraced has been rooted in us for a long time.

Chains of Iniquity

If we have embraced a sin for years, it becomes a stronghold in our lives. Also, strongholds can exist where we have inherited a particular iniquity. These are commonly referred to as **"chains of iniquity" (Jeremiah 16:19, 32:18 and Isaiah 65:7).** For example, one of our parents may have been tormented by worry and fear, so we end up carrying a spirit of fear. Just as physical and emotional characteristics are inherited, spiritual characteristics can be inherited.

How can we handle spiritual problems that we have inherited? How can we change anything we may have received through our natural father and mother? Fortunately, after we are born again, God becomes our spiritual father. As His children, we can take on His character and walk free from any weak or sinful aspects of our parents' nature.

Some have been blessed with a godly heritage through committed Christian parents. Those less fortunate who have received an ungodly heritage have a greater battle overcoming inherited weaknesses. But through the Holy Spirit, we can overcome any such strongholds. **"(For the** weapons of our warfare are not carnal, but mighty through God to the pulling down of strong holds)" (2 Corinthians 10:4).** Since our heavenly Father is good and gentle and temperate and perfect in all respects, we can be transformed into that same nature if we simply yield to His spirit, instead of the old flesh nature that we inherited. God usually delivers us over a period of time, taking different issues in our lives and setting us free as we continue to walk with Him and yield to His leading.

Christians who have been battling inherited weaknesses need to cry out, *"Lord, I despise this sin in my life. Help me to walk free from it."* This cry must be wholehearted because a half-hearted plea will never bring deliverance. **"For I know the thoughts that I think toward you, saith the Lord, thoughts of peace, and not of evil, to give you an expected end. Then shall ye call upon me, and ye shall go and pray unto me, and I will hearken unto you. And ye shall seek me, and find me, when ye shall search for me with all your heart" (Jeremiah 29:11-13).**

As we wholeheartedly seek Him, He will break any chains of iniquity over us, such as fear, failure, insecurity or whatever might plague us. If He can break one chain, He can break them all. As these chains are broken, we will no longer be pulled toward the old things that have kept us in bondage. We will walk free from inherited weaknesses and receive our true inheritance from our heavenly Father.

Expect to Overcome

Unfortunately, we have been taught to expect to be sinners. We have been told, *"Since we are born in the flesh, we are going to fail, and we are going to sin."* With this thinking, it is no wonder most Christians keep on sinning. Upon failing, the response too often is, *"I am just a sinner in weak flesh."* But God has told us to walk in the Spirit, not the flesh. **"There is therefore now no condemnation to them which are in Christ Jesus, who walk not after the flesh, but after the Spirit. For the law of the Spirit of life in Christ Jesus hath made me free from the law of sin and death" (Romans 8:1-2).**

Instead of expecting to sin, we need to expect to be perfect (mature in Christ). Jesus taught, **"Be ye therefore perfect, even as your Father which is in heaven is perfect" (Matthew 5:48).** Our goal is to follow in His sinless footsteps. **"For even hereunto were ye called: because Christ also suffered for us, leaving us an example, that ye should follow his steps" (1 Peter 2:21).**

In our daily Christian walk, we should expect to be following in His footsteps. We should expect not to sin, but to overcome. We must remember if God is able to deliver us from *one* sin, He is able to deliver us from *all* sin. We should anticipate love, joy, peace, health, and all the covenant promises. We must rely on the mercy and grace of God to set us free instead of just accepting we are going to keep on sinning.

Analogy of the Overcoming Walk

By analogy, when we get into a car, we expect it to take us to our destination. We expect the car to run. Although we have a spare tire in case of a flat, we certainly do not get into the car expecting to have a flat, thus needing to change a tire every time we go riding. Let us likewise *expect* our Christian walk to be one of victory over sin! If the enemy comes in and we fall, we have a spare tire (mercy and forgiveness). God does not leave us stranded if a tire blows out or goes flat. He has made provision; a way we can correct any problems. **1 John 1:9** promises, **"If we confess our sins, he is faithful and just to forgive us our sins, and to cleanse us from all unrighteousness."** Confessing our sins is like putting the spare tire on the car. Upon confessing our sins and asking forgiveness, we can keep on moving with God. Instead of sitting by the side of the road in discouragement, we can get up and go on.

Unfortunately, some Christians do not know what to do when, figuratively speaking, their car (their life) breaks down. So, they end up with an old, broken-down car that they do not have to accept. Too many have resigned themselves to failing situations, thinking such thoughts as, *"Well, I guess God wants me to be sick because it will somehow bring glory to Him."* The way God will get glory is for us to be healed and travel on down the road for Him! How can we evangelize the world if we are sick in bed? How can we help others walk in victory when we desperately need help ourselves? However, we do not have to stay in defeat. We do not have to be stuck with a broken-down car. God is able to repair it or give us a new model.

When we are "born again" we receive the new model. We enter into the covenant blessings and walk free from the curse. Let us *expect* the blessings! Let us expect our whole household to be saved. Let us expect to walk in peace and joy and victory. Of course, Jesus said in the world we would have tribulation, but He has overcome the world. **"These things I have spoken unto you, that in me ye might have peace. In the world ye shall have tribulation: but be of good cheer; I have overcome the world" (John 16:33).** We all will encounter problems on this earth, but that is not our expectation. Our expectation is victory. In the same verse that Jesus spoke of tribulation, He added, **"... but be of good cheer; I have overcome the world" (John 16:33b).**

Continuing with our car analogy, we know our vehicle periodically needs to be taken to the filling station. Our spirit man, likewise, needs to be continually filled with the power of God. Too many Christians expect their spirit man to keep on running without ever receiving more of His infilling. We all quickly run out of gas if we are not consistently seeking Him through the Word and prayer. We will hit empty and be stranded at the roadside.

Our car may have a full tank of gas, but what if we are overdue for an oil change? Down the road, we are going to break down. It is the same with our spirit man. If we neglect what we must do to be overcomers, we will break down. Those who break down may cry, *"Oh God, why have you left me abandoned?"* God could respond, *"Did you read the owner's manual? It instructs you to change the oil periodically; it tells you how to maintain our car. It tells us what to do in case of a flat tire."* Some might reply, *"Lord, I cannot even change a flat."* God is so gracious, though, that He will even cover that lack. If we simply pray, He will send someone to help us. He will not leave us stranded on the roadside if we just call on the name of Jesus.

When people are stuck at the roadside, they sometimes think such problems are God's fault. They blame God for the misfortunes that are from their own neglect, or even from Satan. They may even curse God. In their distress they should instead cry out to God all the more, *"God, help me! I do not understand this mess, but I do know You love me and want to set me free."* God's response to our prayer could even be to give us, figuratively speaking, a whole new car.

God gives good things! **"Every good gift and every perfect gift is from above, and cometh down from the Father of lights ..." (James 1:17a).** We have a wrong concept of God if we think He brings bad things into our lives. He does not want us broken down by the roadside, for we are limited as to how we can do our work for Him in that place.

God can redeem bad situations, but people sometimes think He must have caused the problem in the first place. For example, we may have led someone to salvation while we were at the roadside. But that certainly does not mean God caused our breakdown so we could witness. It is simply that He is able to use any circumstance we are in and cause it to work for good. **"And we know that all things work together for good to them that love God, to them who are the called according to his purpose" (Romans 8:28).**

We do not have to be hospitalized to witness to someone there. It is far preferable to walk into the hospital in perfect health and share the Lord. God is not the cause of our being hospitalized, but He can use us while we are there lying in the bed. He can better use us when we are healthy.

God's Word Brings Victory

One reason that many Christians sit at the roadside is because they never realize who they are "in Christ" or "who Christ is in them." They are unaware of their privileges and blessings under the new covenant. Of course, Satan works to keep them deceived. He does not want them to know they are to be overcomers. This lack of knowledge is dangerous, for the Word says, **"My people are destroyed for lack of knowledge …" (Hosea 4:6a).** What knowledge is Hosea referring to? He is referring to the knowledge of God's Word. Christians who are ignorant of the Word are like the driver who does not know how to change a tire; they can sit stranded for a long time. Many Christians do not know the Word well enough to take their next step. It is because they have put everything else in their spirits but God's Word.

Many Christians have a diet of secular TV, secular magazines, gossip and who knows what else. When these Christians encounter a trial, the last thing they may think of is the Word of God. To continue the tire analogy, in fear a person might say *"I am stuck with a flat tire late at night! What am I going to do now? I could be robbed! I could be killed!"* They think such thoughts because they lack the knowledge of God's Word.

On the other hand, Christians who have absorbed God's Word react in faith saying, *"I praise You in the midst of this situation, Lord. I ask for Your strength in changing this tire, and for any necessary help. Thank You."* When those who know God's Word encounter a problem, they do not panic; they maintain their peace because they know Christ's words: **"... In the world ye shall have tribulation: but be of good cheer; I have overcome the world" (John 16:33b).**

In my own life, I was ignorant of an important part of God's Word for many years. Unaware of God's promises of healing, I spent years in such ill health that I reached the point that I was taking 12 different kinds of medication. After receiving the baptism of the Holy Spirit, I came to realize God's promises included healing. My professional medical knowledge (at that time I was a medical lab technician), worked against my faith. However, as God's Word came alive to me, my intellectual knowledge took second place to the knowledge of God's Word. Knowing God could heal me, I had hands laid on me and was prayed for and instantly I was totally healed! My doctors did not understand when I told them God had healed me. They thought I now had mental or emotional problems too, but God simply told me to pray for them. Praise God, later some of the doctors in the clinic were baptized in the Holy Spirit and they too received divine healing.

The proof of my healing became evident in my life when I did not have to return to them for treatment. In the next two decades, following that healing, I did not have to return to a doctor for sickness. During that period of time, Bud and I praised God for His healing hand upon us. This is not to exalt myself, but to exalt the Great Healer and His true Word. God has used doctors in my life at times, since then, to assist in healing. Nothing is wrong with going to a doctor when God is leading you to do so; however, there is a more excellent way. That way is to walk in divine health and that is what we are now striving to do. Each of us must find God's pathway of healing for our individual circumstances.

God's Word is true. At times, Satan has tried to put sickness on me, but I have used the Word of God to battle that foe. Every time I apply the Word of God to a problem, I have been able to overcome. Some battles are short and some are long. I do know that in my own strength I cannot win any of them. Alone, we are no match for the devil. The only time we are a match for him is when we are wearing God's armor. (The armor of God is covered in Chapter Four.)

God's Word Separates

Because God's Word is truth, it separates or divides. People either receive the truth and walk in it, or they walk away from it because as the truth convicts them, they refuse to change the way they are living. Jesus said, **"Think not that I am come to send peace on earth: I came not to send peace, but a sword. For I am come to set a man at variance against his father, and the daughter against her mother, and the daughter in law against her mother in law. And a man's foes shall be they of his own household" (Matthew 10:34-36).**

What did Jesus mean? He meant that if we follow Him, we may be in conflict with those we love, if they refuse to adhere to God's Word. As we continue walking with God and praying for them, they may catch up later, as they mature and make a commitment to Christ themselves. But, if we hold back going forward in how God is leading us spiritually, so that it would keep us from obeying Christ, we will stay in the same place they are spiritually. This could cause us to end up losing the place God is calling us to walk in. For an example if a husband wants a wife to sin with him, she must say "no." She can, and should, submit to him in cases that do not involve breaking a commandment of God; but she must stand against all things that are sinful, even if her husband or family wants her to partake of it.

Separation has even occurred in heaven. **"And there was war in heaven: Michael and his angels fought against the dragon; and the dragon fought and his angels, And prevailed not; neither was their place found any more in heaven. And the great dragon was cast out, that old serpent, called the Devil, and Satan, which deceiveth the whole world: he was cast out into the earth, and his angels were cast out with him. And I heard a loud voice saying in heaven, Now is come salvation, and strength, and the kingdom of our God, and the power of his Christ: for the accuser of our brethren is cast down, which accused them before our God day and night. And they overcame him by the blood of the Lamb, and by the word of their testimony; and they loved not their lives unto the death" (Revelation 12:7-11).**

Satan and his angels were separated from heaven and cast into the earth. Note that on the earth Satan **"... deceiveth the whole world ..." (v. 9).** None of us have been exempt from Satan's deception. It is only as we are "born again" through salvation and continue to walk with the Lord, that we come out of deception into truth. Once we have the Spirit of Christ, we see things that deceived us and the lies that we believed for years are revealed.

Victory Through Humility

Many people though, are not willing to admit that they have been wrong. Pride keeps them in deception. If they are unwilling to confess they were deceived, then they will continue to believe the lies of the devil.

We must always be willing to admit to error. To walk in truth, we have to keep a humble, teachable spirit. Consistently I pray, *"Lord, if I have embraced any lies or deception, show me, so that I might repent of my error and walk in the truth."* God will reveal His truth to us as we yield to Him in this manner. The key is to remain teachable and childlike; not arrogantly assuming that we know it all.

I know just enough of God's Word to realize that I know nothing compared to what is in the Bible. The revelations in God's Word are so deep and so wondrous that we barely receive glimmers of them in this life. I thank God for the glimmers He has given me, and for my being able to share those revelations with others. If there is anything that blesses others through me, it is only through His gift of teaching that He has bestowed upon me. I make no claim to being a good teacher in my own strength. Without the anointing of God, I have absolutely nothing to share. Only His anointing brings life.

I pray this introduction to personal spiritual warfare will encourage readers to ask for a personal heart cleansing in order to prepare them for the greater warfare ahead. May we walk in Christ's humility which paves the way for His power and victory.

PERSONAL SPIRITUAL WARFARE

Chapter 2
Victory Through the Blood of the Lamb

Understanding the Blood's Provision

Revelation 12:11: "And they overcame him by the blood of the Lamb, and by the word of their testimony; and they loved not their lives unto the death." How can the saints of God overcome the devil? **Revelation 12:11** tells us the way to overcome is **"by the blood of the Lamb."** It was the shedding of the blood of Jesus on the cross for our sins that resulted in a multitude of blessings that became available to us. When Jesus rose from the dead, we were given victory and power over our enemy, the devil, and all of his demons.

God's Word makes it clear that the power is in the blood of Jesus. No wonder most cults and false religions are "bloodless." They do not mention His blood; they do not sing about His blood, nor do they spiritually apply His blood. Yet, when Jesus died on Calvary, it was His shed blood that redeemed us from our sins.

First and foremost, the blood of Jesus brings us redemption. **Hebrews 9:22** says, **"And almost all things are by the law purged with blood; and without shedding of blood is no remission."** By the blood of the Lamb, we are redeemed out of darkness into light, out of the kingdom of Satan into the kingdom of God. In the Old Testament, the Israelites were commanded to shed the blood of a lamb (or other animal) to make atonement for their sins. In the New Testament, Jesus was the spiritual representation of that lamb that atoned for the whole world's sins.

Before any of us accepted Christ, Satan was our master whether we knew it or not. We may have thought we were free to do whatever we wanted, but in reality, we were under Satan's dominion. God's Word teaches us that we are all in darkness, serving Satan until we come to Christ. There are only two possible masters we can serve. If we are not serving Christ, we are serving Satan. If we are not part of God's kingdom, we are part of Satan's kingdom. It is only as we accept Christ that the enemy no longer has authority over us.

When we are redeemed, we are given authority. It is crucial that we understand our authority over the wicked one. As joint heirs with Jesus Christ we have been given the same authority He has, an authority that makes our victories possible. **"And if children, then heirs; heirs of God, and joint-heirs with Christ; if so be that we suffer with him, that we may be also glorified together" (Romans 8:17). "Wherefore thou art no more a servant, but a son; and if a son, then an heir of God through Christ" (Galatians 4:7).** If we neither understand nor appropriate the authority we have been given (thereby remaining ignorant), then we are just like those who have no authority.

To walk in victory, we need to heed **James 4:7: "Submit yourselves therefore to God. Resist the devil, and he will flee from you."** Our responsibility for victory is to submit to God and resist the devil. If we do this, he must flee because **"... greater is He that is in you, than he that is in the world" (1 John 4:4b).** We have victory over Satan to the degree we are submitted to God. If we are totally submitted, then we can have total victory over Satan.

Deception, Ignorance and Rebellion are Destroyers

As we stated earlier, there are three major areas where people are overcome by the devil: ignorance, deception, and rebellion. As Christians, however, we have not been left powerless against this enemy. We have been given redemption and authority, all through the blood of Jesus.

Our enemy has only one major weapon: *deception*. The only way he can defeat us is by deceiving us into agreeing with his lies. He is able to deceive many Christians because they are ignorant of the Word of God. It is as **Hosea 4:6a** says, **"My people are destroyed for lack of knowledge …"** Of course, this is not referring to worldly knowledge, but rather knowledge of God's Word. Good Christians are being destroyed simply because they do not know what God's Word says about their situation. Deceived Christians do not realize that the devil is under their feet, not vice versa.

Through deception, Satan causes people to believe that evil things are good. To them "black is white" and "white is black." He fools them into thinking that his way is better. It is not only ignorance of the Word that causes people to fall for this lie, but also, by yielding to the desires of their own flesh that they will come to destruction as well. Satan causes people to call "good" evil and "evil" good. **Isaiah 5:20** says, **"Woe unto them that call evil good, and good evil; that put darkness for light, and light for darkness; that put bitter for sweet, and sweet for bitter!"**

Satan also instigates rebellion against God. Some have rebelled to such an extreme that they have deliberately decided to follow Satan rather than God. Thus, we are seeing more and more occult groups participating in blatant satanic worship. Christians shake their heads and wonder why people would deliberately worship the devil. But people do so because they are deceived and full of rebellion.

The Blood Cleanses

We do not need to be overcome by the enemy because the blood of Jesus has paid for our victory. What the blood of Jesus does for the body of Christ has many comparisons as to what human blood does for the natural body. My former occupation was a medical lab technician and one of the main things I did was to conduct lab tests on the blood of patients. Examining a person's blood can reveal if a person is healthy or if they have a disease. Human blood plays a vital role in the health of any individual. This being the case, I want to use an analogy of how the blood of Jesus brings life to us as Christians, just as human blood brings life to a person in the natural realm.

The blood's cleansing ability is of primary importance. As human blood circulates, it gathers impurities. These impurities are brought to the heart, lungs, kidneys, colon and liver for disposal. In the lungs, the blood exchanges carbon dioxide, an impurity, for fresh oxygen. This is why blood from an artery is bright red, while blood from a vein is dark, almost blackish red. The blood in the veins is carrying impurities back to the heart and lungs, while the arteries carry oxygen and nutrients to the entire body. This is how cleansing and healing takes place in the body through human blood.

Likewise, the blood of Christ cleanses us spiritually. **1 John 1:7-9** says, **"But if we walk in the light, as he is in the light, we have fellowship one with another, and the blood of Jesus Christ his Son cleanses us from all sin. If we say that we have no sin, we deceive ourselves and the truth is not in us. If we confess our sins, he is faithful and just to forgive us our sins and to cleanse us from all unrighteousness."** The blood of Christ cleanses us from all sin so that we can come before God with clean hands and clean hearts. Cleansed by Christ's blood, we can come boldly before the throne of God.

The devil may yet accuse us of sinfulness and unworthiness, but the promise is that if we have confessed our sins, we are not only forgiven but also cleansed of all unrighteousness that is caused by the sin. Therefore, we can boldly enter into the holy of holies to receive what is rightfully ours. Should the enemy try to undermine our faith by telling us that we are terrible, unworthy sinners, we can stand on God's Word and say, *"Satan, in Jesus' name, I refuse your accusations. I am acceptable before the Lord because He has cleansed me. I have confessed and repented of my sin, so I am clean."*

Perhaps we are trusting God to answer a prayer when along comes Satan saying, *"Remember that lie you told this morning. God is not going to give you anything because you are a liar."* Then those who do not adequately know the Word might lose their faith saying, *"Yes, I did lie, so I guess I do not deserve anything from God."* Of course, in our sinful state we do not deserve anything. However, if we have confessed and repented of our sins, we can say, *"Satan, I have confessed that lie to God; therefore, I am cleansed and can receive what is mine in Christ. You will not prevent me from receiving what I have prayed for, in Jesus' name."*

Upon our confession and repentance of sins, God is even able to turn around the consequences of our sins and use them for our good. **"And we know that all things work together for good to them that love God, to them who are the called according to His purpose" (Romans 8:28).** As we repent of our past misdeeds to God and surrender completely to His will, He is able to take those wrongs and use them for our benefit. What a master planner He is! What the enemy would use to destroy us; God uses for our good. It is important, however, that we do our part, which is to give our sins to God and ask Him to somehow bring good out of the wrong we have done. This is known as God's redeeming work. Sometimes the good that comes is simply a lesson for us not to go in the way of sin again. I know of many people who went to prison for deeds that they did before they came to Christ and many times God caused the parole boards to release them early since their lives were changed by God while they were in prison.

We must understand that it is by His righteousness and not our own, that we are made acceptable. **"... There is none righteous, no, not one" (Romans 3:10b).** Therefore, we can come before Him only in His righteousness; by what His blood has done for us. Because our righteousness is based upon Christ's perfect work for us, we can boldly declare that God's promises are ours. We never need to say, *"I do not deserve anything because I have sinned."* For if we have confessed and turned from our sins, we are made righteous.

However, if we do not confess and repent of our sins, the answers to our prayers may be blocked. It is not so much that God will withhold from us, but rather that our own rebellion will prevent us from receiving. We will reap what we sow. Because of this, we need to stay pure before the Lord and understand that the blood of Jesus cleanses us from all sin when we repent of our sins. **"But as for them whose heart walketh after the heart of their detestable things and their abominations, I will recompense their way upon their own heads, saith the Lord GOD" (Ezekiel 11:21).**

Life in the Blood

The blood of Jesus also provides eternal life. If it were not for His sacrificial blood, we would not have life in the spirit. Likewise, human blood is the key to life in the natural body. **Leviticus 17:11a** says, **"The life of the flesh is in the blood**

..." The body can function only as long as it has a sufficient quantity of blood; if we lose too much blood, we die.

Incidentally, one segment of the medical profession claims that life is in the spine. This is not so; for the Scripture says that life is in the blood. There are also many medical practices that have their roots in witchcraft. The enemy seeks to bring *new age* doctrines and practices into the medical field. Christians who submit themselves to such treatments ignorantly open their spirits to *new age* thinking. This *new age* theology is a form of witchcraft and partaking of it can bring the spirit of witchcraft against us. Involvement with such techniques as acupressure and acupuncture can hurt us spiritually, as these stem from Eastern religions. We need to be careful in choosing a doctor. To avoid opening our spirits to the wrong thing, we need to pray for guidance as we seek out caring doctors.

God wants us to eventually reach the place that we can receive healing directly from Him. Until we do, He certainly will not be angry if we seek medical assistance. There is nothing wrong with going to a physician but pray about your choice of doctors.

Healing in the Blood

Besides cleansing and life, the blood of Jesus brings healing. **1 Peter 2:24b** says, **"... by whose stripes ye were healed."** Through the stripes that Jesus took on His back (by the soldiers who were whipping Him) and the blood He shed at Calvary, we have physical healing available to us. Many Christians do not realize we can receive healing from God. For years I did not know that Jesus shed His blood for my salvation and that salvation included my healing. After I was filled with the Holy Spirit, God began to show me that He wanted to heal me. When I received prayer for healing, I felt God's power. The pain left my back and body. Knowing that I was healed, I threw away my medication. God leads all of us differently, but you will know what you are to do if you ask God for His advice. We must individually find God's pathway to our healing. Be certain of your healing before you stop taking prescribed medications.

God wants us to be healed. When I was healed, it was glorious! It was wonderful to be free from all those infirmities. Before my healing, I had a chronic case of sinusitis. I took habit-forming codeine for the severe sinus pain. I also had back trouble, nervousness and phobias. I was taking pills constantly. I had 32 allergies for which I received weekly shots. I was so allergic to dust I could not even clean my own house. God healed me of every single one of those infirmities.

Healing comes from God, and sickness comes from the devil. The devil would love to make us allergic to everything to deny us the good things that God wants us to enjoy, whether it is certain foods, or plants, or animals. If we accept the enemy's lie and his allergies, then he can keep us in bondage with an allergy. For example, if we believe that we are allergic to cats, every time we are near a cat, the enemy can bring an allergic reaction. But we can be free from allergies if we believe the Word of God. The Word says nothing shall by any means hurt us **(Luke 10:19)**. We need to know that we have power over allergies, or any infirmity from the enemy.

Off and on over the years, my late husband, Bud, suffered from asthma. After he became Spirit-filled, his asthma problems ceased. However, when we were traveling as evangelists and visiting in a home with cats, Bud again experienced an asthma attack. All night long we prayed against the physical assault, but the healing did not come until we left that house. We declared, *"No, Satan, Bud is not allergic to cats. It is you causing this and we reject it."* A month later the same thing happened in another home with cats. Again, we said, *"We tear down Satan's stronghold."* Yet, Bud's relief did not come until we left that house. Two weeks later at a third home we went through the same sequence of events. But we kept declaring God's Word.

The enemy has a strong case when he shows ongoing evidence in the natural realm. He works on the natural senses to convince us of his lies. Bud saw the cat, he touched the cat, and he began wheezing.

Finally, at the fourth home with cats, Bud had no asthmatic reaction. He was totally healed, and never again had a bad reaction to cats. It took three battles to bring down Satan's stronghold. Our minds could have convinced us that cats were the problem, but the actual problem was Satan with his deception. God's Word is always greater than the problem. Bud's healing was complete, and we were able to have pet cats in our home!

When we did missionary work in India and Africa, we were cautioned to be very careful about what we ate or drank. Those who travel to foreign lands typically pick up parasites or foreign bacteria and suffer from dysentery. As a medical lab technician, I viewed parasites under a microscope. I knew how people got them, their life cycles, about their hosts and so forth.

When we were invited to eat at someone's home, I knew of the health dangers, especially since most of the homemakers in the foreign field lacked knowledge of sanitation procedures. But I also knew God's Word said to eat what is set before you when you go forth **(Luke 10:8)** and that if you drink poison, it will not harm you **(Mark 16:18)**. The food had been prepared for us with love but in a filthy kitchen, so

I believed God's Word above my medical knowledge. We enjoyed that blessed meal with no ill effects and spent 30 days in that area without suffering any dysentery. Where sanitation laws are not yet understood, God's higher law of love can cover you. God's Word is true if we believe it over the natural circumstances. We always say the blessing over our food before we eat, no matter where we are and God cleanses it to the nourishment of our bodies. While traveling all over the world, we ate in many restaurants and have never had food poisoning because we always pray over our food before we eat it.

Of course, this does not do away with proper sanitation. Typically, missionaries teach sanitation procedures, if necessary, when they go into villages where the residents are ignorant of proper sanitation and food preparation procedures. Valuable rules of hygiene are found in the Old Testament, along with rules about safety procedures, foods to eat and avoid, and so forth. These physical laws are written for our benefit and certainly are not meant to be discarded; however, when we cannot prepare our own food, we can trust God to cleanse the food we eat.

Strongholds Broken by the Blood

Over the years of our lives, we receive the lies of the enemy because we do not know the Bible and God's ways, so we build up ungodly strongholds in our minds. A stronghold is anything that **"... exalteth itself against the knowledge of God ..." (2 Corinthians 10:5a).** A lie of the enemy, if not rejected, can become a stronghold. For example, if we believe that every winter we can contract flu during that season, then we will be open to sickness. The truth is, that in Christ, every season is one of blessing and health. Bud and I prayed every fall before the winter season, and we spiritually inoculated ourselves from the flu by declaring that the enemy is defeated and we are protected from all flu viruses. The Lord has been faithful to protect us without flu shots. I have only had to battle a flu attack once or twice over the years.

Sometimes we have to battle to win over strongholds. After my initial healing several decades ago, there have been occasions when I have had to declare God's Word over sickness that would try to come upon me. Because God is faithful and His Word does work, in all these years I have rarely had to return to a primary doctor for illness. We mainly went to the doctor for our annual check-ups. Since our marriage, my husband Bud only rarely had to go to a doctor until his death at 93 years old. We are not exalting ourselves as faith giants, but rather God's Word as being true. Yes, we have had some health battles over the years, but we can declare that Jesus, our great physician, always brought healing to us either through a doctor or divine healing from God. We praise God for His faithfulness and exalt Jesus the healer!

In overcoming strongholds, one tool we have is the blood of Christ. His blood has cleansed us so that we can say, *"I am clean, Satan, so you cannot put sickness on me. I do not receive it."* We may be in pain or have symptoms of an illness, but as we declare God's Word of healing, those things must flee.

Sometimes the healing comes immediately, other times we have to battle. I have been instantly healed, but I have also had to fight overnight, for days, or even months. Right now (at this writing), I am in a battle that is several years old, but I know I will see victory through Christ because His Word is true.

We are not advocating the Christian Science teaching which is "mind over matter," but rather, that the Word of God is greater than Satan's sickness. Pain and sickness are real; they do exist and are not just in our minds. However, we are declaring the greater existence of God's healing power over these attacks of the devil. We are declaring that sickness has no right to exist in our bodies because our life in Christ Jesus has made us free from the law of sin and death. Sickness is a death principle. **Romans 8:2** says, **"For the law of the Spirit of life in Christ Jesus hath made me free from the law of sin and death."**

The way to victory is not by someone else's experience, but by personally applying what the Word says. The Word will come to pass if we are surrendering all to Him, walking in obedience to His principles and believing Him. God never fails! We are the ones who are prone to failure, but He helps us to overcome.

Strength is in the Blood

We are meant to overcome, and God provides us with the strength to do it. Strength is another thing that comes through the blood. The Bible says, **"... be strong in the Lord, and in the power of His might" (Ephesians 6:10b).** Strength is ours as Christians. Weaknesses are from the enemy. He tries to wear us down physically, emotionally and spiritually so he can overtake us. But God says to be strong in the power of His might.

Thank God He did not say, *"Betty, be strong in your might."* In the natural realm, I am one of the weakest persons imaginable. Weak and fearful, that was me before I knew Jesus. But when God told me to be strong in His might, I called on Him and He gave me strength.

We are to call on Him. When we are weak, He is strong. There have been mornings when I awakened and felt too weak to get started or even make it to the Sunday morning church service. But I have learned to say, *"Deliver me from this weakness, Lord, and give me strength to do Your will today. Give me strength to overcome right now."* God has never failed to provide that strength when I had need of it. To God be the glory!

Through God's power, in the many years we ministered together, Bud and I never missed a meeting because of sickness or weakness. (Before marrying Bud, I missed one meeting at a time when I was still learning how to walk in faith.) There have been times that I have thought, *"Lord, I am so weak today; You are going to have to give me Your strength."* Then I would move in faith and find God strengthening me for the next step - and the next one - throughout the day. As I trusted Him step by step, I became both victorious and faithful to God because of His strength in me. Faith is just taking one more step with Jesus until you walk into your answer.

Too many Christians use anything as an excuse not to do the Lord's work. They may say that they have a headache. Instead, they need to resist headaches, weaknesses or emotional depression. There have been occasions when depression has hit me and I have thought, *"Lord, I do not feel like ministering to these people today."* Because so many Christians go by their feelings, they are stopped in their service when they "do not feel like doing it." Instead, they need to say, *"Lord, I am not going by my feelings; I am going by Your Word which promises Your strength and might. Give me Your strength to minister."*

Do you know what God often does as I ignore my feelings and go to minister? He ministers to me as I reach out to meet another person's need. There have been times when I have been hurt by someone and have felt like hiding in self-pity.

Then God would thrust me out to minister, despite my struggles. He caused the self-pity to lift.

Self-pity is dangerous. We have to stop it before it grows. If we do not, the enemy can even carry it to the extreme of suicide. Some have thought that we have lacked compassion when we have said to someone strongly to resist their self-pity. But this is actually the kindest thing we can tell that person; we are speaking the truth in love **(Ephesians 4:15)**.

We dare not succumb to the emotions of self-pity, resentment, anger, grief, bitterness, hatred or any such negative thing, as we can drown in them if they overtake us. It is not sinful to have negative emotions, but they are temptations which can allow them to rule us and in turn they can overcome us. If we open the door to these thoughts and dwell on them, the enemy can come in like a flood and destroy us with depression, despair, fear and torment. For years, I never experienced deep discouragement, but then I got a full dose of it. At that time, I had to resist that evil emotion because the enemy wanted to destroy me with it. If we see destructive emotions tormenting an individual, we should tell them as kindly as we can, *"You need to let go of the anger, bitterness and/or resentment or it will destroy you."*

As we stay close to Jesus, who is our spiritual strength, we can overcome negative feelings. We can talk honestly to the Lord about these feelings. He already knows anyway. We can say, *"Lord, I am angry, but I know I should not be. Please help me deal with this anger. Remove it from my heart."* We can tell Him when we are discouraged and need His encouragement, or tired and need His strength.

Strength is provided in the human body through hemoglobin in the blood. If we are low in this iron compound, we will become anemic and thus lacking in strength. Spiritually, we receive our strength through the blood of Jesus as we follow the Lord.

The Blood Brings Nourishment

His blood also provides spiritual nourishment, just as human blood nourishes us by carrying nutrients to all parts of the body.

If we do not stay close in our relationship with Jesus, receiving His nourishment, we will become spiritually anemic. We will lose our strength. There are too many Christians who do not maintain their relationship with Him and do not feed on His Word. Instead, they feed on "spiritual junk food."

What does it mean to eat "spiritual junk food?" It is taking in that which the world has contaminated. A lot of people read books, magazines and watch hours of TV but never read the Bible, through which the Holy Spirit could minister to them.

Acts 20:28 says, **"Take heed therefore unto yourselves, and to all the flock, over the which the Holy Ghost hath made you overseers, to feed the church of God, which he hath purchased with his own blood."** In this admonition to pastors, God is saying, "Feed My people so they can grow in Me." There are Christians who think they can feed on "spiritual junk food" and still grow in Christ. They cannot, as they will become weak and anemic.

I appreciate Christian literature. We have written numerous Christian books and pray that they bless people, but there is no substitute for the Word of God. Reading Christian materials and listening to Christian sermons is good, but if all we ever do is feed on these materials to the exclusion of the Bible, it is like having a constant diet of processed baby food or instant TV or microwave dinners. The real unprocessed spiritual food is the pure Word of God.

God has made preachers and teachers available to us, as well as Christian videos and teachings, books and study aids, to help us grow in Him. But this should be only part of our diet, not the whole of it. Such Christian food can sustain us temporarily, but we must include daily study and prayer times with God. We need the meat of the Word; we need to allow the Holy Spirit to illuminate the Scriptures directly to our hearts.

What God wants most is a close relationship with us. If we do not take time for that, we will never know the joy that He has for us. We have to take the time to be with Him.

For the best conversations, husbands and wives usually require one another's full attention. They can discuss matters as they are busy with other tasks, but deeper communication requires more. At times, when I have been working in the kitchen while talking to Bud, he has said, *"Honey, can you set aside what you are doing and sit with me to talk?"* The kitchen task was a distraction to our conversation.

Many Christians talk to Jesus throughout the day, but they never sit down and give Him their undivided attention. If we need that full attention in human relationships, then Jesus needs it as well. Let us give Him a chance to speak to us. And let us not make it a one-sided conversation saying, *"Oh Lord, give me this; do this for me; help this person and do that."* Requests are fine but let us also take the time to let the Holy Spirit minister to us. Let us include, *"Lord, is there something You want to reveal to me today? Are there any changes I need to make in my life? Is there something I am going to face today for which I need preparation? Show me by Your Word what I need for today. Is there something on Your heart, that you want me to pray for or something I need to do for you?"*

The Blood Provides Protection
 So much has been made available to us by the shed blood of Jesus. Another provision from the blood is protection. **Exodus 12:13** says, **"And the blood shall be to you for a token upon the houses where ye are: and when I see the blood, I will pass over you, and the plague shall not be upon you to destroy you, when I smite the land of Egypt."** Before leaving Egypt, the Israelites were instructed to put lamb's blood on the sides and at the tops of their doorways. Blood was not to be put on the threshold because it was symbolic of Christ's blood, which could not be trampled upon. We cannot walk upon the blood of Jesus. It is over us and protecting us, just as the lamb's blood over the Israelites' doors protected all within their households when the death angel passed over them.

His blood is our protection, but we should not make a fetish out of it. Some Christians in a rote fashion confess, *"I claim the blood of Jesus over this. I confess the blood of Jesus here; I put the blood of Jesus there."* Just saying these words, using His blood this way, is like using a fetish that repels evil. This is a wrong approach. When we apply the blood, we must apply it by faith. It is *faith* in what the blood has done for us that brings protection, healing and strength, not the mere confession of His blood.

I have heard Christians say, *"No devils can come in here because we have surrounded this place with the blood of Jesus."* Yet the place is swarming with demons because their heart attitudes are wrong, and faith is lacking. Again, it is the blood of Jesus applied by faith and our obedience to

43

Christ that brings protection. That is what will protect us from the death angel, the plague, and all that the enemy would bring against us.

Sometimes we are unaware of God's protection. In heaven, I believe we will be surprised, as we see the number of times God protected us from harm. Some of us can already testify of incidents when God rescued us just inches from disaster, fully protecting us from the wicked one's schemes.

One incident of God's protection over me occurred years ago when I was working in the medical lab. I had just recently been filled with the Spirit and healed; in my excitement, I would witness to anyone who would listen. One doctor said, *"What's happened to Betty? She's in the hospital halls preaching to everybody."* I was simply eager to tell what God had done for me. One day a salesman came into the lab where I worked. I started witnessing to him, but he was not receptive. I tried witnessing a few more minutes; still nothing was affecting him, so I said, *"Would you let me pray for you?"* As I laid my hand on his shoulder in prayer, I felt a powerful anointing fall on me. I thought that God must be planning to use this man in a mighty way. I had never felt such an anointing. But the man departed; seemingly unchanged. I thought, *"Lord, the anointing was so strong; something should have happened to that man."* As I went about my work, God spoke to me, *"I gave that anointing to protect you. That man has an evil, wicked heart and is full of demons. He is not ready to come to Me. Because you are so open, you could have unintentionally opened your spirit to the demons in him. I protected you from that."* I later learned the man was a womanizer who constantly made advances toward females. I was single at the time, and God protected me from the man as he never bothered me again. Even when we do not realize it, God is protecting us.

The Word Brings Victory

Revelation 12:11 says, **"And they overcame him** (Satan) **by the blood of the Lamb, and by the word of their testimony; and they loved not their lives unto the death."** If we are going to overcome the enemy, we must first have a relationship with Jesus. We must be redeemed by His blood. We should use the Word of God as our testimony, as it is not about what we have done, but what He has done in our lives. This does not mean we overcome simply by our personal testimony, such as the one I gave about my healing. Instead, it is the testimony of the Word of God and what it produces in our lives. It is our testimony of what God's Word has done for us and is not about what we have done for Him.

The Bible is made up of the Old and New Testaments. It is Jesus' last will and testament, an inheritance left for us. The Scriptures are His testimony. These are the Words that overcome the enemy. It is not *our* words that overcome. We could quote ourselves all day long and it would have no effect on the enemy.

However, as we quote God's Word against the devil, he has to flee. God's Word is the sword of the Spirit by which we battle. We need to find out what the Word says about our situation and then confess that Word over our problem. In this way, we will overcome. We need to tell the enemy, *"Satan, the Word says, 'By His stripes I am healed.' Jesus died on the cross that I might be whole. You will not prevent me from receiving my inheritance, in Jesus' name!"*

Some may wonder how we dare talk this way to the devil. We speak this way, because God has made us His sons and daughters. We are not being prideful; we are simply appropriating what Christ did for us. It pleases God to see His children receive their inheritance. It delights Him when we receive healing. He died so we could have His blessings.

I do not want His death to be in vain. I want to be among those who will receive all that He died for.

How does He feel when we do not receive what He has made available? It must break His heart when His people stay defeated, weak, in bondage, and sick all the time because we do not appropriate what is ours. God is saying, *"Receive it. Walk in it. It is yours!"* Jesus Himself overcame the devil by quoting the Word of God to him. **"And Jesus answered and said unto him, Get thee behind me, Satan: for it is written, Thou shalt worship the Lord thy God, and him only shalt thou serve" (Luke 4:8).**

Dying to Self Brings Victory

Along with the blood of Jesus and the word of our testimony, victory is dependent upon our loving not our lives unto the death **(Revelation 12:11).** We will never gain victory until we reach the point that we would rather die than ever deny the Lord Jesus. We have to come to the place where we die to ourselves so that He might live in us. This is total commitment.

We will never have much victory until we are totally committed to the will of God. If we are only 90% committed and obedient, the 10% in which we are uncommitted and disobedient will open the door for the enemy to destroy us. We have to come to a place of total submission if we are going to do anything for God. We should be able to say, *"I had rather die than hurt or deny my Lord and sin against Him. Oh, Lord, take this sin out of me; cleanse me. I had rather die than bring reproach on Your kingdom."*

With that attitude of dying to ourselves so that He might live in us, we will overcome. As we die to our way and allow Christ to live in us, we gain victory because He is never defeated. He cannot be defeated; so, if we allow Him to fully live in us, we cannot be defeated. But it is our choice. That is why so many Christians are defeated; they have never made a total surrender of their will to the Lord.

Total commitment says, *"I will go anywhere, give up anything, stay anywhere or do anything that God asks."* It is God's responsibility to give us the strength and ability to do whatever He has called us to do. That is His department. We commit—and then He provides.

We will never be disappointed or regret that we fully submitted to the One who created us. He has the greatest plan for our lives. We will be so fulfilled and enjoy His plan so much that we will never be sorry. He is simply waiting to bless us with every desire of our heart that is good and righteous. **"Delight thyself also in the Lord; and he shall give thee the desires of thine heart" (Psalm 37:4).**

He wants to remove every wicked desire from our hearts. He will do this for us if we yield to Him. We cannot lose if we trust Him! He will remove from our hearts the wrong desires that are hurting us, and then He will be sure to fulfill the righteous desires that remain.

God loves us. He loves everyone! But only those who commit to Him completely will overcome. These are the ones who love not their lives unto the death, who use the Word against the enemy, and who receive their righteousness through the blood of Jesus. If we want to be among these overcomers, the place that we must start is with a total commitment and submission to God. Then we shall have victory through the blood of the Lamb. This is a "must" in order to win our spiritual battles.

PERSONAL SPIRITUAL WARFARE

Chapter 3
Requirements for Good Soldiers

Obedience is the First Requirement

Our warfare is spiritual. We are not wrestling against flesh and blood, but against principalities and spiritual wickedness in high places.

"For we wrestle not against flesh and blood, but against principalities, against powers, against the rulers of the darkness of this world, against spiritual wickedness in high places" (Ephesians 6:12).

Our battle is not against human beings, but against Satan and his demonic powers. To win this battle, we must be good soldiers in Christ. And to be good soldiers, we must meet certain requirements.

Good soldiers are determined to win; to be overcomers. Remember the three overcoming keys from **Revelation 12:11**: **"And they overcame him by the blood of the Lamb, and the word of their testimony; and they loved not their lives unto the death."**

1.) We overcome by the blood of Jesus
2.) We overcome by the Word of God
3.) We overcome by being totally committed to God unto death

First, we overcome by the blood of the Lamb. We are redeemed and filled with the power of the Holy Spirit, so that we can walk in His power, not ours. It is the power of God that brings our victories. Jesus sacrificed his life on the cross as the "Lamb of God" in order that we might receive

49

forgiveness for our sins and receive the life and power of God so that we can overcome all things. When Christ rose from the dead, He made a way for us through the Holy Spirit to walk in victory if we receive His plan for our lives.

Secondly, as good soldiers walking in His might, we wage war with the Word of our testimony. That Word is the Scriptures, not our own human words. It is speaking God's Word that puts the enemy to flight, not speaking our own human thoughts or giving our own personal testimonies. The Bible is composed of the Old and New Testaments so the testimony that we overcome with is the testimony of the Word of God. Certainly, a part of that testimony is our personal testimony of how the Lord personally saved us as individuals, but it is the Word of God that carries the power of God for our needed victories. Jesus, Himself, overcame the assaults of the devil by using the written Word of God to defeat the devil. Jesus spoke the Word of God to him in **Matthew 4:7: "Jesus said unto him, It is written again, Thou shalt not tempt the Lord thy God."**

Thus, as good soldiers we are to put our emphasis on the Word of God. We know that His Word brings victory. Whether the problems are financial, marital, emotional, or any other kind, we need to find out what the Bible says about that issue. Then, we can apply that Word to our situation and gain the victory. We war by praying the Word of God over our situation and by being obedient to the Word of God through the power of the Holy Spirit.

Marriages fail because couples ignore God's principles. They are living selfishly, doing their own thing. God's way, however, is to lay down one's life for another; that is true love. Such love does not come automatically; it is both taught and learned. Emotional feeling for another is only one part of marital love. The Bible tells older women to teach younger women how to love their husbands. Spouses must learn to love with God's love. A teachable spirit is a must for this.

Titus 2:4-5: "That they (older women) **may teach the young women to be sober, to love their husbands, to love their children, To be discreet, chaste, keepers at home, good, obedient to their own husbands, that the word of God be not blasphemed."**

The third thing we must do to walk in victory is to make a total commitment to God. This means we must be willing to do anything, go anywhere or give up anything for the cause of Christ. Good soldiers are 100% committed and obedient to God's Word. A 90% commitment will not win the victory, for the enemy will use the 10% lack to contaminate the portion given to God. Good soldiers know that total victory comes only through total commitment and obedience.

Where full commitment is lacking, Christians receive only temporary relief from their problems. They may attend church, receive prayer, and walk away with temporary relief, instead of the total recovery that God has available for them. Temporary relief is like tearing off the top of a weed but leaving the roots. Getting to the root of the problem for total recovery requires total commitment and total obedience. Partial obedience is *not* obedience.

Of course, good soldiers **"... loved not their lives unto the death" (Revelation 12:11b).** This means we are to die to our own desires and ways and live unto the Lord's ways. We should have an attitude of preferring death to hurting Jesus or disobeying God. It can take many years for some Christians to reach this point, although it is available at conversion. Those who do, totally commit on a daily basis, lead lives of joy, victory and peace.

Christians can be divided into two groups: overcoming Christians leading lives of victory, and defeated Christians enduring lives of defeat. It is not that one group is more favored by God than the other. The Bible says that God is no respecter of persons.

Acts 10:34: "Then Peter opened his mouth, and said, Of a truth I perceive that God is no respecter of persons:"

Colossians 3:25: "But he that doeth wrong shall receive for the wrong which he hath done: and there is no respect of persons."

It is simply that the victorious group applies and obeys God's Word in their lives. God is not favoring them; He is favoring His Word. Since He is partial to His Word, if we line up with it, we will automatically receive favor and blessing. The only advantage that one Christian has over another Christian, is the knowledge of God's Word and the application of that same Word. You can be a child of God and experience destruction in areas of your life if you lack the knowledge of God's Word or fail to apply it to your life.

Hosea 4:6a: "My people are destroyed for lack of knowledge: because thou hast rejected knowledge, I will also reject thee ..."

Defeated Christians are those who do not live according to God's Word. They tend to be plagued with problems that are never solved. All Christians, of course, experience problems, but the good soldiers learn to overcome them with joy. Instead of constantly being under a load of problems that prevent them from accomplishing all that God has for them, good soldiers will be finding the solutions and eventually getting their needed victories. This means getting victory over character defects as well, such as fear, jealousy, greed, lust, anger, etc.

The root of the problem for many Western Christians is the lack of desire to serve the Lord at all costs. Believers in countries where Christians are persecuted know what it means to serve at all costs—even at the cost of their lives. That is the kind of determination required of good Christian soldiers. We are to *love* God more than we *fear* man.

If the day should come in America that religious freedom is denied, we would quickly see the separation of true Christians from the phonies. Even at the threat of death, true Christians will still serve Jesus. Though we have not been put on the line in this way, we are put on the line in our hearts when we take a stand in our hearts by saying that we would rather die than sin against God or yield to the world's standards.

Living by God's Standards
Good soldiers live by God's standards. Therefore, it is crucial that we not be ignorant of what God has to say, as I was for many years in the area of healing. I was not healed until I learned that healing was God's standard.

We should desire God's standard in every area of our lives. Recently, our church went through a difficult financial battle. Mainly, we wanted to win that battle because the Word says, **"Owe no man any thing, but to love one another ..." (Romans13:8a).** God's standard is to be free from debt. We wanted to line up with His Word, and not just be relieved of financial pressure. Good soldiers check every area of their lives to be certain that they are lined up with God's Word, whether it is their marriage, their children, their

53

church relationships, their diet, or their finances. Good soldiers want everything they have to be under the authority and dominion of the Lord!

When I first began to study the Bible, I was often shocked at what I discovered. Finding a new truth in the Scriptures, I would think, *"Lord, am I supposed to be doing this? I have never done this in my life!"* Then I would ask God for His strength to line up with His Word. I would pray, *"Oh God, I did not know this was a sin."* In our hearts, we sometimes have a feeling that what we are doing is wrong. When we are able to see the confirming truth in God's Word clearly revealing it as sin, we will then know the truth and the truth will set us free. At that point, He will empower us to make the change if we ask Him to. It is His desire and good pleasure to help His children be like Him.

John 8:32: "And ye shall know the truth, and the truth shall make you free."

I remember hearing a message that pointed out a sin I had been participating in. Surprised, I asked the Lord to forgive me and deliver me from that sin. I had not even seen my sin because I was so influenced by the world's way of thinking. The world has told us that black is white; that it is all right to do such deeds. **Isaiah 5:20: "Woe unto them that call evil good, and good evil; that put darkness for light, and light for darkness; that put bitter for sweet, and sweet for bitter!"**

When the world says something is not sin, but the Bible says it is, good soldiers listen to God's truth. For example, our American society says abortion is fine; God's Word calls it murder. We have to check society's standards against the Word of God. We cannot do what society approves of, if God's Word does not approve of it.

To be good soldiers, we need to study the Word, allowing it to become absorbed within and become an actual part of us. After all, when a crisis hits, we will not always have time to search the Scriptures for a solution. If we have not already absorbed the truth within; it is not going to be what we respond with. The computer abbreviation GIGO (*garbage in, garbage out*) has application to us. If we program garbage into our hearts and minds instead of God's Word, garbage will be all that comes when a crisis hits.

For example, consider the Christian in a marriage crisis who spends days gazing at soap operas that constantly depict couples getting divorces, lacking in faithfulness and chastity, and showing no forgiveness. As the Christian's marriage comes under pressure, the apparent solution is what the couple in the latest soap opera did: divorce. That is "garbage in, garbage out." It is escaping the problem, rather than applying God's principles to overcome the problem.

A whole generation, particularly in America, has been negatively affected by television. They have been brainwashed into accepting worldly standards. This deception has even extended into the churches where many are preaching a compromised gospel, a watered-down version rather than the full truth. Many people live together and are not married. They no longer think this is wrong and have now accepted this worldly standard. The Bible calls it fornication.

As compromise is tolerated, the church ends up acting just like the world. No wonder the church's divorce rate is as high as society's. Instead of applying God's principles to remedy a bad marriage, Christians are following the world's escape route. Yet, God has provided a way to overcome any problem we face, if we will fill our hearts and minds with His Word. We can never get too much of His Word.

Soldiers who neglect the Word of God will end up backslidden. Years ago, that was my condition. One of my first mistakes was to quit reading the Word. Oh, I still prayed a little. You know how we are; we still want to talk to God. When I did open the Bible, I found my standards had slipped. If I had stayed exposed to the Word, it would have served as the plumb line to keep me lined up with His standards.

That is why it is so important to read and study the Word, to hear the Word expounded at church, to listen to Christian messages, and so forth. If we are straying, the Word acts like a compass pointing us back to the standard. Without consistent exposure to God's Word, the standard that holds us steadfast, we can drift out of His will and straight into sin.

It is so easy to drift away from the positive things of God. For example, if we do not fellowship where faith is preached, our faith can start to slip. If we go where messages are full of doubt and compromise, then we will walk in doubt and compromise. Wise soldiers will seek fellowship where the messages are ones of faith, of overcoming, of laying down one's life for Jesus. As that standard is held before us, we will be conformed to it by the work of the Holy Spirit. God's Word is the anchor that keeps us from drifting away from His standard.

Steadfastness Needed for God's Victory

Spiritual victories can take time. Let us not be discouraged when answers are not immediate. Sometimes, we may gain instant victory, but other times it can be days, months, or even years. I had to pray for 20 years before I saw my father saved. Do not give up. Keep walking in faith and believing God for your answers. God is faithful.

For many years, as I prayed for my father, I was unaware of how to war in the Spirit. Basically, I just cried out, *"Oh God, save him. Oh God, save him."* When I came into a Spirit-filled walk, I realized that evil spirits were blinding my father from the truth. One day, as five of us were in prayer, the Lord spoke for me to fast and pray for my father. We spent the day doing that. Three months later, God sent me to visit my father who was then ill. It was time to witness to him.

When it comes to witnessing to relatives, most of us experience some difficulties. But as we have faith in God, in His timing He will fill our mouths. Do not hesitate; it is no different from witnessing under God's unction to a stranger.

As an example, the powers of darkness were keeping my father from being saved. However, before I spoke to him about salvation, I asked five of my praying friends to agree with me that he would be saved soon. After we prayed in tongues for a time, we felt a release, as we felt the Holy Spirit would prepare his heart to receive. Prayer had broken the evil spirit's hold on him. I sensed a holy boldness the next time I spoke to him and was able to speak to him about the condition of his soul. I said, *"Daddy, you are very ill right now with gout. If the doctor gave you a pill, saying it would remove all sickness and pain, you would take it, wouldn't you?"* He said, *"Well, of course."* I said, *"There is a pill you need to take: it's the "gos-pel" of the Lord Jesus Christ. If you will make Him Lord of your life and ask Him to forgive you of your sins, He will wash away all this burden of sin you have carried for years."* Daddy started crying; I started crying, and he accepted the Lord. We both sensed the Spirit of God. My 20 years of praying had mounted up, but the most effective prayer had been when the five of us used these spiritual tools:

Tools of Warfare

1. *Fasting* (We were fasting that day.)
2. *Agreement* (There were five of us praying together that day.)
3. *Travail* (Our day of prayer included this travailing or crying from our hearts to God.)
4. *God's Word* (That day we confessed appropriate salvation Scriptures over my father.)
5. *Resistance to the devil* (We spoke God's Word against the enemy telling him to leave my father according to **James 4:7.**)

As we applied these tools, the barriers broke down. Our spiritual warfare opened my father's heart and mind to the truth.

We need to wage war in the spirit to free our loved ones. Good soldiers will enter into spiritual warfare to tear down the powers of darkness that blind the unsaved. The Bible says Satan has blinded the minds of unbelievers preventing them from receiving the gospel. **"In whom the god of this world hath blinded the minds of them which believe not, lest the light of the glorious gospel of Christ, who is the image of God, should shine unto them" (2 Corinthians 4:4).** We can witness to a loved one all day long, but until the spirits blinding him are defeated, they cannot truly hear. It took spiritual warfare before my father could finally hear and receive.

The morning after my father's salvation, the enemy attacked me with the thought, *"Your father did not really get saved. He was just humoring you, saying that prayer so you would leave him alone."* I prayed, *"Lord, confirm his salvation experience to me."* I got a Bible for him and took it to his home. I said, *"Daddy, you need to read this daily, pray daily, and attend a good church."* He responded, *"Betty, I already prayed this morning."* Since he had received salvation, Holy Spirit had already prompted him to pray. I did not have to tell him that - Holy Spirit did! Thus, God confirmed his salvation experience for me. Other changes also came, such as he no longer used curse words.

Good soldiers do not give up. Let us not give up on our relatives, no matter how much spiritual warfare it takes. My father could have seemed like a hopeless case as he was the black sheep of the family, but through God's love, he was saved.

I pointed out earlier that God is no respecter of persons. Neither is Satan. **1 Peter 5:8** says, **"Be sober, be vigilant; because your adversary the devil, as a roaring lion, walketh about, seeking whom he may devour."** The devil does not care whom he devours, just as long as he can get somebody. He is seeking "whom" he may devour, which means there are those he cannot devour. If we are good soldiers wearing our spiritual armor, being sober and vigilant, then we cannot be devoured. Unprepared Christians, however, can be devoured by the devil. He has ruined the lives of many believers. Jesus spoke of what the devil, as a thief, does in this verse.

John 10:10: "The thief cometh not, but for to steal, and to kill, and to destroy: I am come that they might have life, and that they might have it more abundantly."

Soldiers Resist the Devil

Since the Bible says the devil goes about as a roaring lion, we need to know that his roar is empty noise. He has no power or authority against us, if we stand in our place of authority in Christ. Too many Christians do not realize this, so they cringe at his roar. Because they do not resist his attack, these fearful Christians are devoured. But those who know the Word and their position in Christ will roar back at the devil. They will resist the enemy and declare, *"Satan, in Jesus' name, I resist you. I raise the Word of God against you. By God's power I declare you are not going to destroy my marriage or my loved ones. You will not rob me of my spiritual inheritance. In Jesus' name, I declare that you will not take away my love, my joy nor my peace."*

Take notice the devil "acts" *as* a roaring lion. The *real* lion is on our side, "The Lion of Judah" (Jesus). Greater is the Lion in us than the "counterfeit lion." The devil constantly imitates. He has no original ideas, but counterfeits what God has done; even counterfeiting the gifts of the Holy Spirit at times.

For example, he tries to give counterfeit peace. He calls his demons back from their assignment, and that person feels peace in the sense that he is no longer under demonic assault. Satan uses that tactic to keep people in a compromising position, to keep them from battling through to victory. Satan stops bothering them for a season; so they stop crying out to God.

Cessation of assault may bring a temporary relief, but only the Holy Spirit can bring true peace to our hearts. With His peace inside of us, we can remain calm no matter how hard the storms rage around us. It is not so with the world— their peace is dependent upon agreeable circumstances.

Good soldiers need to know the truth. **1 Peter 5:9-10** says, **"Whom** (the devil) **resist steadfast in the faith, knowing that the same afflictions are accomplished in your brethren that are in the world. But the God of all grace, who hath called us unto his eternal glory by Christ Jesus, after that ye have suffered a while, make you perfect, stablish, strengthen, settle you."**

We know several things from this Scripture. First, that suffering and affliction come from Satan, not God. Satan is the one who brings suffering; he is the one who assaults us. Second, we can be encouraged with the knowledge that our brethren have experienced the same trials we suffer. No one has been spared the enemy's afflictions. Third, we can be assured that if we endure the suffering and remain steadfast in the Word, then after a season we will be made perfect, strengthened and settled. God will bring us to that place of steadfastness where we will no longer be overcome by the enemy. There are two kinds of suffering - suffering for our own sins and suffering for Christ. God wants to deliver us from sin and the suffering that goes with it, and He will give us the grace to endure and overcome the suffering that comes because of our obedience to the Word of God.

What is our goal? Certainly, it is not to remain in a place of suffering or sickness. Some Christians mistakenly think that their suffering is their cross to bear. God does not want us resigning ourselves to suffering with some sort of "grin-and-bear-it" attitude. He wants us to overcome it. Our goal is to overcome as we resist the enemy. Thus, we are made perfect in God; steadfast, strengthened, established and settled.

Stand fast against sickness. Stand fast against demonic assault. Resist the enemy with the Word of God. Yes, we will have affliction: **"... In the world ye shall have tribulation ..." (John 16:33b)**, but that same verse carries these words of comfort: **"... but be of good cheer; I** *(Jesus)* **have overcome the world."**

We must keep our eyes on Jesus. We cannot let the problem loom so large that it overwhelms us. That is Satan's plan - to hit us with a problem that seems impossible to solve. Then we feel helpless and that all is hopeless. In this defeated condition, people can even be susceptible to suicide spirits.

But if we know who Christ is in us, the moment we encounter a problem, we will view it as an opportunity for God's glory to be manifested as He provides the victory. By resisting the enemy and submitting to the Lord, we can turn every satanic assault into glory for God. We will come into this place of strength and victory after we have suffered a little while. We will suffer some while going through a battle. The purpose is not in the suffering itself, but suffering is the route that perfects, establishes, strengthens, and settles us. Then, we can walk in strength and not be shaken by the enemy's attacks. When he roars, we roar back, unshaken.

Having passed through the suffering unto victory, we know the same God that delivered us the last time will deliver us this time as well. His Word is still true. **1Peter 5:9** says we **"... resist steadfast in the faith ..."** By faith we resist and overcome. **James 4:7** also mentions resisting: **"Submit yourselves therefore to God. Resist the devil, and he will flee from you."** The *"will flee"* is a guarantee; it does not say that he *might* flee - it says that he *will* flee!

Soldiers as Watchmen

Watchfulness is required of every good soldier. In an army, any soldier designated as watchman on night duty dare not fall asleep. He stays awake, ever alert watching for the enemy. As Christian soldiers, our watchfulness includes checking out the orders to be certain that it is God speaking, and not the enemy trying to deceive us.

The enemy will often send along something that appears good; it may seem to be a positive thing and in the will of God. But, if we are alert soldiers, we will seek the Lord on the matter. Since the enemy wants to sidetrack us with concerns that will rob us, drain us, take our time and even destroy us, it is essential that we check to make sure we are getting our guidance from Holy Spirit and that it is God speaking to us.

The enemy can be a crafty foe. He knows that once we are totally committed to God, we are going to resist overt sin. He knows we will not be behaving as the world does, so generally he does not waste his efforts trying to trip us up with obvious sins. Instead, he resorts to presenting us with a plan that looks like it is God's plan. If we do not examine it before God, we might fall for it. We might assume it is the way God wants us to go. Then, halfway down the road we wonder why everything is turning out so wrong. It is because we never thoroughly checked with Him beforehand. We were not watchful. In the Old Testament, before his battles, David "inquired of the Lord." He never fought a battle without God's guidance and instruction.

For example, consider the area of inviting needy people to stay in our homes for a while. As Christians, we are to be generous and minister to the poor and needy; but we must be led by God's Spirit. Sometimes the solution is an invitation to come and stay with us, but other times God will provide a different answer. If we are always motivated by guilt that says, *"I am a Christian so I need to invite them in,"* then the devil can have us operating out of human sympathy and overloading us with tasks that are not of God. We cannot be led solely by our natural sympathy; we need the compassion and wisdom of God.

Because I had a sympathetic nature, for years the devil was able to overload me with burdens that the Lord did not want me to bear. I would think, *"Well, if I do not help here, I am a bad Christian."* I wore myself out trying to minister to everyone's needs, when God only wanted me to minister to certain ones. Satan tries to wear us out so much that we do not even have the strength left to help those God really wants us to help.

Of course, there are situations that certainly require us to provide Christian help. For example, we would not leave a friend stranded by the roadside. But there are other needs that the enemy brings before us that require that we carefully seek God's direction as God has other plans for this person. We must seek the Lord, so that we do not fall into one of Satan's traps.

Obedience and Holiness

Just as watchfulness keeps the enemy from sneaking in, so obedience and holiness keep the enemy from breaking into our lives. Obedience and holiness are essential parts of a good soldier's armor. **1 Peter 1:14-16** says, **"As obedient children, not fashioning yourselves according to the former lusts in your ignorance: But as he which hath called you is holy, so be ye holy in all manner of conversation** (behavior)**; Because it is written, Be ye holy; for I am holy."** We are exhorted to be holy in all of our lifestyle, holy like our Father. God would not ask us to do something we could not do. As we yield to Christ, we can be holy through His holiness worked within us. Holiness is something imparted to us as we walk in the Spirit.

Obedience and holiness seal off the enemy from access to our lives. Many Christians have doors wide open to the enemy. The devil does not have to find a crack to squeeze through; he can walk right in! Disobedience has caused the door to be wide open. If we are disobedient to what God speaks, we are leaving an open door for Satan. He can then come and go as he pleases. Therefore, it is crucial for us to obey God's Word.

Disobedience, which is rebellion, gives the enemy the right to enter into our lives. When we do this, we lose our God given rights and our position of authority. How could a battlefield soldier survive if he disobeyed orders? Or what if he stayed hidden in a foxhole refusing to do his job? He would never be part of the victory. What if he thought that he could handle the enemy all on his own? Attacking alone, he would be killed. If a Christian soldier is hiding out or trying to battle in his own strength, he will be overcome.

By ignoring their Commander's orders, many Christians are ministering in their flesh, rather than in the spirit. Thus, they are overwhelmed by Satan as they involve themselves in supposed good works that God has not called them to do. In their misdirected zeal, they say, *"I am going to do this for God, and I am going to minister here for the Lord."* In the meantime, their own personal lives are in shambles, their families are not being ministered to, and their finances are a mess. Yet, they keep declaring that they are going to minister for God. Their first ministry is to get their own homes in order, to straighten out their own lives. Until that is done, they dare not be out on the front lines where the enemy could wipe them out. They cannot yet handle a ministry because it first requires obedience to God and the ability to handle spiritual warfare. Ministering for the Lord takes more than desire and zeal.

At the other extreme are the do-nothing Christians. They are the ones covering their heads in foxholes. They are protecting themselves but accomplishing nothing. Eventually the enemy runs them over, too. Either extreme will end in disaster. The only way we will have victory in personal spiritual warfare is through watchfulness, seeking and heeding His commands, and through holiness and obedience.

1 Corinthians 9:7: "Who goeth a warfare any time at his own charges? who planteth a vineyard, and eateth not of the fruit thereof? or who feedeth a flock, and eateth not of the milk of the flock?"

Endurance and Discipline

Good soldiers also learn how to endure hardness. **1 Timothy 1:18b** says, **"... war a good warfare."** War is hard work; any war requires enduring some hardness.

2 Timothy 2:3: "Thou therefore endure hardness, as a good soldier of Jesus Christ."

First, there is boot camp. Here, soldiers learn strict obedience, discipline, and the strategy of war. Can you imagine a boot camp trainee saying, *"Sir, how about breakfast in bed?"* Some Christian soldiers act like that when they cry out, *"Oh God, give me this, give me that. I want a big new car, Lord, and a new house. I claim this; I claim that."*

Such Christians, expecting God to serve their every want, are not true soldiers. They foolishly treat God like a bellhop that they can signal, *"Come wait on me, God, come wait on me."* They seldom, if ever, ask the Lord what He would have them do for Him that day.

We will never be good soldiers until we have the attitude that says, *"Here I am, Lord, use me in service unto You."* We are here to serve God, not vice versa. Of course, if we have a valid need, we can ask, and God will surely respond. We do need a place to live, and transportation and God wants to bless us by furnishing them for us; but we need to be sure we hear Him as to where He wants us to live. A battlefield soldier might ask for more ammunition. God will certainly supply more ammo if we ask for it.

God will make sure we are equipped to serve Him. He is the perfect leader; the best we could ever follow. As the commander in chief, He has access to an unlimited expense account, meeting all of our needs. In everything that He has called us to do, He has always furnished a way for me personally, given me favor, and paid for all He instructed me to do. He is always there to take care of His soldiers.

God, the commander in chief of His Army, is concerned about us, as His soldiers. He will show us how to attain victory in our personal lives. As we learn how to win our personal battles, He then wants us to start winning battles for others. Our purpose is to help others attain victory in their lives, too. We help others, and others help us. Many times, I have felt, *"Lord, I cannot fight this battle any longer. Raise up intercessors, Lord. I need prayer support."* If you reach that place where you can no longer battle alone, ask God for the intercessory help that you need. He may tell you to call a certain fellow soldier or He will put your name on someone's heart so that they will pray for you. I have done that and received the necessary reinforcement that I needed. As we stay sensitive to the Holy Spirit, He will provide the necessary ammunition, strength and help.

We are guaranteed victory in every battle we go through, if we obey God. That is an important *"if."* If we obey God, we cannot lose. It needs to be so real to our spirits that we are on the winning side. The devil is the loser. We only lose if we fall into disobedience or rebellion.

Romans 8:31: "What shall we then say to these things? If God be for us, who can be against us?"

As we engage in spiritual warfare, our heart attitude must be one of faith and victory. We cannot be complaining, *"Oh*

God, why have You left me here in such a difficult spot?"
Instead, the proper faith attitude says, *"Lord, I am growing weary but give me Your strength and reinforcements. Help me, because I want to be Your overcomer and bring glory to Your name."*

Do you see the difference? When pressure mounts, we have two possible responses. We can complain, whine and succumb to our circumstances, or we can say, *"Lord, give me Your help and strength to overcome."* The choice is ours. Let us say, *"Although I cannot do it, Lord, I know You can do it through me."*

I have had sessions like that, crying out on the floor before God. But God has always made a way for me through His power and His might. **Ephesians 6:10b** points out that *it is His might*, not ours: **"... be strong in the Lord, and in the power of his might."**

2 Timothy 2:3b says, **"... endure hardness, as a good soldier of Jesus Christ."** The trying of our faith takes place when our situations become difficult to bear. God knows when we are being tried. And if we are still praising and trusting Him, our attitude is precious to Him. **"That the trial of your faith, being much more precious than of gold ..." (1 Peter 1:7a).** As we stand strong through a rough battle, God knows we are doing it because we love Him.

When the road has been rough, I have sometimes said, *"Lord, I have never had it as rough as You did. You had nails in Your hands, stripes on Your back, and a crown of thorns on Your head. My suffering is so little compared to Yours."* Remembering what the Lord endured always makes my load feel lighter.

Then too, consider the suffering church around the world! In certain foreign countries, Christians are heavily persecuted, crammed into filthy prison cells, and tortured for Christ's sake. Few of us have had to endure such hardships. We are fortunate that our sufferings are so light. Considering that, we can pray, *"Lord, we will not complain about our situation. Thank You that we have it as easy as we do."* A grateful attitude will bring us through our battles even more quickly.

The devil wants to drive us deep into depression. His plan is to get us to curse God and give up. As circumstances go from bad to worse, most people at least feel like giving up and abandoning God. Job's wife advised him, *"Curse God and die."* But Job still followed God. Later, he realized God was not the one afflicting him; it was Satan. Through it all, he learned he had a problem with self-righteousness and pride. When he repented of standing on his own righteousness, God restored to him double what the enemy had taken.

We can easily fall into spiritual pride or self-righteousness, thinking, *"Why is this happening to me? After all, I have done absolutely everything God's required of me. There is no sin in my life!"* This very attitude can reflect pride and block what God wants to do. We need to say, *"Lord, I have done everything I know to do, but if I am blind to something more, then show me. I know that You have full wisdom and will give me Christ's victory over this."* As we have faith, God will give us any additional information needed to win the spiritual warfare battle.

Avoid Worldly Entanglements
After Paul wrote, **"endure hardness,"** he added, **"No man that warreth entangleth himself with the affairs of this life; that he may please him who hath chosen him to be a**

soldier" (2 Timothy 2:4). If we are going to walk in victory, we cannot be caught up in the things of this world. There are so many things that would take us away from our true mission of serving the Lord Jesus Christ. Some of these things are not sinful in themselves, but if they detract from that which spiritually strengthens us, then we could lose the battle.

Take a sport for example. Bowling is not sinful, but what if our involvement is such that we are neglecting prayer or Bible study time? Missing that time of spiritual strengthening could result in our losing a spiritual battle.

There are times for our involvement in non-spiritual activities, but they should not be so consuming or competitive that we miss how God wants to use us during that activity. God may have us go bowling in order to witness to someone. Wherever we go, we are to be a light. Sometimes the Lord sends us out as lights to a world that would otherwise not be reached.

Avoiding entanglement with the world does not mean we only read the Word and stay in prayer. We can certainly engage in other activities but let us make sure that it is not the enemy diverting us from spiritual priorities. He is out to spiritually drain us. If we are in a war, we cannot be wrapped up in non-priority activities. We need to stay in an attitude of spiritual warfare and be led by the Lord in all areas.

God may call us to sacrifice hobbies for the sake of His kingdom. We must be sure that what we are doing fits God's plan for our time. Then too, after a season of warfare, God may provide a hobby for a season of rest. Our God is not a hard taskmaster.

Some ministers have been overcome because they never learned to rest. They kept firing cannons, constantly on the go, always in an attitude of warfare, warfare, and more warfare. They would have been more effective if they had also included periodic strengthening seasons of rest. Even soldiers in the world are given "leave" for a sabbatical.

Some do all the battling and refuse to rest; others do all the resting and refuse to battle. Both battling and resting are needed to walk in balance with God. As we are led by the Spirit, we will know what season we are in. If it is a season of battle, we certainly cannot entangle ourselves with worldly affairs. We have to avoid distractions and focus on the things of God.

Striving for Victory

Continuing in **2 Timothy 2:5**, Paul says, **"And if a man strive for masteries, yet is he not crowned, except he strive lawfully."** Consider one application of this Scripture: we cannot preach or teach a truth that we are not personally walking in, or striving (working) to attain by His rules. If I were to teach on how to gain Christ's victory but did not apply it to my own life, then I would not be striving lawfully. I would be a hypocrite.

Good soldiers lawfully obtain their blessings according to God's pattern. We cannot expect God to bless us when we are not doing things His way. We must be obedient to Him and His principles if we are to obtain spiritual blessings.

As we prove our obedience, God will give us greater responsibilities. With greater responsibilities come greater privileges. These are needed to offset the extra time required by our duties. So, God gives us favor and help. If He asks us to do something more, and we think, *"No more; I cannot possibly take on anything more,"* He will make a way. He may lighten our load in another area or provide us with additional help.

God will never require more of us than we can handle. If we think that we are unable to do something, we can pray, *"Lord, You called me to this, but I do not feel qualified. I need Your help and strength. Either do the necessary work in me or send someone who can help."* Often, homemakers feel burdened with the challenge of raising children and spending quality time with them along with their other household duties. But God will lighten their load as needed. We can trust Him in all these things.

God is so good. One of the enemy's major deceptions is fooling most people into thinking that God is mean, that serving Him and battling for Him will be so difficult that they will never be able to overcome. The enemy has people thinking, *"Only those saints in leadership can overcome, not I."* The truth is that God has made it possible for *all* of us to be victorious.

Dying in Order to Live

Jesus said, **"... If any man will come after me, let him deny himself, and take up his cross, and follow me. For whosoever will save his life shall lose it: and whosoever will lose his life for my sake shall find it" (Matthew 16: 24-25).** Denial of self is a key to victory. **Revelation 12:11b** says the overcomers **"... loved not their lives unto the death."** This is contrary to the world's thinking. While Jesus says one has to lose his life to gain it, the world tells us to look out first for "number one." The world says that to be successful, you must position yourself first, even if you have to step on others as you climb the ladder of success. God, however, says that success comes through being the greatest servant, denying oneself, and promoting, ministering to and thinking about others. This is the way that we gain in the kingdom of God. We gain by losing.

Unfortunately, most couples do not apply this principle to their marriages. We see two selfish people refusing to budge, both wanting things their own way and both expecting the other to wait on them and serve them. Until they learn to serve one another, their marriage will be a failure. What a person gives, he receives. As the song goes, *"Love is not love until it is given away."* We cannot expect to receive love until we give it out.

Good soldiers deny themselves and take up the cross daily. We need to know just what our "cross" is and what it is not. It is not the unsaved spouse, nor the unruly kids, nor the financial pressures. These things are not our cross. Instead, our cross is denying *self-will*.

We have a choice: to keep our will or to surrender to God's will. This is our cross - the point where our will conflicts with (crosses) God's will. Then we have to deny ourselves and say, *"Lord, I yield to Your will."* Daily, we take up our cross by yielding our will to His, even when it is not what we want to do. That is where we die to self. Learning what God wants us to do is part of bearing our cross.

"I beseech you therefore, brethren, by the mercies of God, that ye present your bodies a living sacrifice, holy, acceptable unto God, which is your reasonable service. And be not conformed to this world: but be ye transformed by the renewing of your mind, that ye may prove what is that good, and acceptable, and perfect, will of God" (Romans 12:1-2).

Learning to turn the other cheek, go the second mile, to minister yet again to someone we have helped numerous times before, this is all a part of carrying the cross. And what if the Lord asks us to go beyond the second mile? That cross is ours to bear so we yield our wills to His. When we take up this challenge daily, yielding our wills to His, we will be good soldiers.

Jesus said, **"If ye were of the world, the world would love his own: but because ye are not of the world, but I have chosen you out of the world, therefore the world hateth you" (John 15:19).** Good soldiers are not popular in the world. But we have been chosen to come out of the world and serve God. It is a commitment the world cannot understand and a lifestyle they even hate. But we have chosen to be good soldiers. I pray that we will all ask God to strengthen us to be good soldiers for Him - to be strengthened to endure hardness and to overcome through Jesus Christ.

PERSONAL SPIRITUAL WARFARE

Chapter 4
The Armor of God

Preparing For Battle
Ephesians 6:10-18 (KJV)

10 Finally, my brethren, be strong in the Lord, and in the power of his might.

11 Put on the whole armour of God, that ye may be able to stand against the wiles of the devil.

12 For we wrestle not against flesh and blood, but against principalities, against powers, against the rulers of the darkness of this world, against spiritual wickedness in high places.

13 Wherefore take unto you the whole armour of God, that ye may be able to withstand in the evil day, and having done all, to stand.

14 Stand therefore, having your loins girt about with truth, and having on the breastplate of righteousness;

15 And your feet shod with the preparation of the gospel of peace;

16 Above all, taking the shield of faith, wherewith ye shall be able to quench all the fiery darts of the wicked.

17 And take the helmet of salvation, and the sword of the Spirit, which is the word of God:

18 Praying always with all prayer and supplication in the Spirit, and watching thereunto with all perseverance and supplication for all saints;

These verses from **Ephesians 6** are well-known by most Christians on the topic of spiritual warfare. It instructs us to **"Put on the whole armour of God."** The cover image of this book depicts this preparation showing the most important position of the soldier which is the bent knee of prayer before battle. Most of us have heard warfare teachings based on these verses, but another look is in order. Anytime we study the Word, it will refresh and encourage us, it will make us stronger, and we may discover truths we have never seen before when we ask God to give us His revelation.

A minister once likened revelation to a tree. When the Lord first gave him revelation on a topic, it was comparable to the trunk of a tree coming forth. As God added to the original revelation, it was like additional branches beginning to grow out of the tree. So, it is with God's Word. We receive revelation and as we continue to study His Word, further revelation is attained. The Word of God has much depth; it contains layers of truth. As we grow spiritually, we discover truths in the Word that we never saw before.

First of all, these verses are an analogy of how to obtain victory through Christ over the forces of Satan. Many people, including some Christians, do not believe there is a devil. For many others, spiritual warfare is a topic to avoid as they are fearful of the devil, not realizing he is defeated. Some, who are compromising Christians, have become apathetic and lazy, as they do not want to think about having to battle through prayer. But when we consider spiritual warfare we must realize that it calls for entering into a fight.

It calls for applying pressure back on the enemy of our souls, Satan, who is constantly applying pressure against us.

We have assurance in this war, assurance unknown in any other war. We are assured of victory; it is promised in God's Word. **"… greater is he that is in you, than he that is in the world" (1 John 4:4b).** All we have to do to win this war, is to apply God's Word and His principles to our battles and walk in obedience to Christ. The Old Testament contains many dramatic examples of victory against impossible odds through obedience. We will win all battles if we seek and perform the will of our commander in chief.

Putting on Our Armor
As explained in **Ephesians 6:10-18**, here are the pieces of our spiritual armor we must embrace:

1. Loins are girted with **truth**.
2. Breastplate is putting on the **righteousness** of God.
3. Feet are shod with the **gospel of peace**.
4. Shield of **faith** is raised against the enemy.
5. Head protected by the helmet of **salvation.**
6. Sword is using the **Word of God** against the devil.

2 Corinthians 10:3 says, **"For though we walk in the flesh, we do not war after the flesh."** Ours is a spiritual battle; not one of flesh and blood. No human being is our enemy. The enemy is Satan with his evil principalities and powers of darkness that work through human beings who are weak or deceived vessels (those who believe his lies). In previous chapters, we have seen that we have authority over these powers of darkness. As we speak to them, they must obey. We have also noted that our victory is dependent upon our total commitment. If we are not sold out unto the death we may as well forget about entering into spiritual warfare.

Battle in the Mind

Where does the battle begin? It begins in our minds. **"(For the weapons of our warfare are not carnal, but mighty through God to the pulling down of strong holds;) Casting down imaginations, and every high thing that exalteth itself against the knowledge of God, and bringing into captivity every thought to the obedience of Christ" (2 Corinthians 10:4-5).** Where are the strongholds? They are in our minds. That is why Paul says we are to cast down imaginations and everything that exalts itself against the knowledge of God as our thinking comes under obedience to Him. Consider this: ultimately, the only power Satan has over believers is the power of deception. For deception to work, one must believe a lie. Therefore, if the devil plants a lie into our minds and that lie becomes a stronghold, we are doomed to be defeated without deliverance.

For instance, what if we believe that God does not want to heal everyone? What if we think He is selective in His healing? Then if we become sick, the enemy will whisper that God heals some, but not us personally. The devil will tell us that we are the exception to the rule that God heals. If we embrace that lie, we will not be able to receive our healing. In this way, the enemy will keep us from victory.

The truth is that God is no respecter of persons. His healing is available to everyone. It is like salvation. Christ died on the cross so that everyone might be saved - _everyone_! But not everyone is saved, because they have not accepted the provision. Christ's provision includes healing as well: **"… by whose stripes ye were healed" (1 Peter 2:24b).** Note the past tense _were_ healed. It has already been done. Legally it is ours. All we have to do is receive it by faith; however, just like salvation has to be received, so does healing. Neither of these gifts are automatically bestowed upon us.

To receive healing, we must come in faith, believing that it is ours, because God has provided it. Otherwise, the enemy will use a stronghold in our minds to rob us of our inheritance. We are to cast down any imagination that the enemy has exalted above the knowledge of the Word of God. That is why we need to know God's Word. Then, when we face trials, the knowledge of the truth will provide whatever we need to overcome the enemy. If the enemy hits us with sickness and follows with the lie, that God put it on us to teach us a lesson, we can then reject the devil's lies with the truth of the Word of God.

God never uses sickness to teach us. He teaches us through His Holy Spirit and His Word. If children in school listen to their teacher and read their textbooks, they learn. But if they do not listen and study, they fail at test time. It is the same for us. If we have been ignoring our teacher, the Holy Spirit, and neglecting our studies, the Bible, we will fail life's tests. But if we have done our homework and the Word has been worked into our spirits, we will overcome. Every time the enemy lies to us, we will counter it with the truth of the Word. Some victories will be instant, while others will require our continually standing on the Word for a season. Because His Word is true, eventually every victory will be manifested if we remain steadfast.

Ephesians 6:10b tells us to **"… be strong in the Lord, and in the power of his might."** In our own strength, we are powerless against the devil. He is a supernatural being - and as human beings we cannot overpower him. The exception, of course, is the human who is "in Christ". In Christ, we have authority over Satan; without Christ, we are already defeated. That is why the world is being wiped out by the enemy. They are defenseless against his assaults on their marriages, their children, their finances, and their health.

God's strength changes us. When I received the baptism of the Holy Spirit, I boldly began witnessing whenever I had the opportunity. I was unashamed of the gospel, whereas before I had been timid about sharing my faith. I was embarrassed to talk about God.

After being baptized in the Holy Spirit, I had a new holy boldness when sharing Jesus with others. This holy boldness is also to be upon us when we confront the enemy. Christians should not fear the devil. Even a newborn babe in Christ has more power over the devil than the devil has over him. The enemy will try to bluff us into thinking that he is to be feared and that we dare not arouse him. He does this to keep people passive, to keep them from pressing into their inheritance in Christ. The devil wants us to ignore him. But does the Word say to ignore the enemy? No! It says to resist the devil, and he will flee **(James 4:7)**. To resist him, we first must identify him. We must know where he is positioned. Some would advise not to talk about the enemy, thinking that such attention brings him glory. It does not bring glory to the devil when we talk about him! We are talking about how to identify, fight and overcome the devil.

James 4:7: "Submit yourselves therefore to God. Resist the devil, and he will flee from you."

Identifying the Enemy

Identification is important. In a natural battle, it is essential to know where the enemy is. Often, he is camouflaged. How does Satan camouflage himself? He tries to look like God. Certainly, he does not approach committed Christians saying, *"Here I am, the devil, follow me."* Committed Christians love their Lord too much to fall for the overt sins. Satan's tactic is to deceive us into thinking that what we are doing or believing, although wrong, is of God. He wants to get us off track. Satan does this, for example, when he convinces Christians that God will heal other people, but He will not heal us.

We need to align our thinking with the truth of the Word. Too many people passively accept what someone tells them about God or their misinterpretation of the Scriptures. Many times, a person's understanding of the Word is in error because of their own carnality, immaturity or lack of commitment. Rather than accept someone else's teaching, we need to go directly to the Bible and find out what it really says. Through the Word and the Holy Spirit within us, we are to check out everything we hear. For instance, we are to examine these teachings in the light of the Scriptures. We should approach God saying, *"Lord, I do not know if that is true or not. I lay aside any pride and humbly ask that You show me the truth in Your Word."* If we approach Him with humble hearts, genuinely desiring the truth, then we will be able to change our doctrine to line up with the Word of God if we have been wrong.

Over the years I have had to lay aside men's doctrines for the truth of the Word. How many Christians have been taught that speaking in tongues is not of God, and that it will only tear a church apart? I have had to search the Scriptures for the truth. If I had not searched the Word, I would have missed out on one of God's most wonderful blessings. I am grateful the Lord gave me the gift of speaking in tongues as promised in the Bible.

One area that requires our searching the Word is in regard to end-time teachings. There is such a variety of teachings on this topic that it might be wise to put it all on the shelf and say, *"Lord, help me to receive only what is of You."* When I received the baptism of the Holy Spirit, I was eager to know everything I could about the end times. So, I gathered together a dozen books on the topic only to find the Holy

Spirit restraining me from reading them. When I tried to read a book, I would either fall asleep or be interrupted by a visitor. Finally, I asked the Lord about it, and He told me most of the material was man-made tradition that He did not want me putting into my spirit. How are we going to know about end times? We will have to humbly ask God to show us the truth and be willing to lay aside any misinformation we already may have absorbed and ask Him to lead us to read only those teachings that are of Him. The Lord warned us there would be false prophets and false teachers in the last days and told us not to be deceived. The only way we can avoid this is to stay close to God and be guided as to where we are to receive teachings from others. We are also to prove all things by the standard of the Word of God.

1 Thessalonians 5:21: "Prove all things; hold fast that which is good."

Warning Against Deception
Ephesians 6:11 says, **"Put on the whole armour of God, that ye may be able to stand against the wiles of the devil."** Our enemy is a wily foe, full of craft and cunning. At one time or another, we have all been deceived by his tricks. **Revelation 12:9b** says he **"... deceiveth the whole world."** Before our salvation, we were under deception, and we all still have varying degrees of deception that we are not yet delivered from. Some are more delivered than others, depending upon how much of the Word has been personally applied to their lives.

We have heard the saying, *"Fool me once, shame on you; fool me twice, shame on me."* The devil may have fooled me the first time around on some things, but not the second. After discovering I had been tricked, I was determined not to fall twice for the same thing. We have all been fooled by the enemy and thereby lost some battles. But if we have made a mistake, let us not get under condemnation. All we need to do is ask God for forgiveness, get back up and go on with Him. If we keep pressing in, eventually we gain the victory. All the while, we should remain watchful for the enemy's tricks. We should be in the habit of checking everything out to be certain that it is the Lord speaking, and not the enemy. I have a saying and that is to run everything through the Holy Ghost filter.

Some areas, of course, do not need to be checked out as the Word of God is very explicit about what we are to do. Unless there is an extreme and dangerous situation, we do not have to pray, *"Lord, should I divorce my spouse?"* The Word is clear about God's hatred of divorce. We do not have to pray about whether to lie, steal or cheat. Such things are obvious. But in the unsure areas, we need to seek the mind of the Lord. *Should we move here? Should we take this step in our job or ministry? Should we purchase this car? Should we marry this person?* By letting God lead, we can avoid mistakes that would bring unnecessary suffering.

Must be Led by the Spirit

God's sons (and daughters) are led by His Spirit. **"For as many as are led by the Spirit of God, they are the sons of God" (Romans 8:14).** This is an essential truth to grasp. If we are led by circumstances or how we feel, by anything less than God's Spirit and His Word, then we are going to be led astray by the enemy.

Too many Christians are led by feeling: *"I do not feel like doing that."* It does not matter whether we feel like it; if God says to do it, we will be able to do it in His strength. **"I can do all things through Christ which strengtheneth me" (Philippians 4:13).** God will give us the strength and power to do His will.

Another group of Christians are led about by circumstances. While circumstances can be a factor in guidance, they are not to be the major criterion. To make them such is putting the cart before the horse. Some would pray, *"Lord, if You want me to go pray for that sick brother, then send a red sports car past my window."* This type of proposal to God can open the door for the enemy to interfere because that is the last car the enemy would let go by your window.

Granted, such fleecing worked for Gideon. **"Behold, I will put a fleece of wool in the floor; and if the dew be on the fleece only, and it be dry upon all the earth beside, then shall I know that thou wilt save Israel by mine hand, as thou hast said" (Judges 6:37).** And many times, God will honor the fleeces of baby Christians because they do not yet know how to hear His voice. But He wants us to grow beyond that level of proposing things to Him, of saying, *"Lord, if such-and-such happens, then I will know to do thus-and-thus."* Instead, He wants us to be sensitive in our spirits to His voice. Once we have received His guidance in our spirits, the circumstances will line up. He will make the necessary provision for us.

For example, we may feel called to minister somewhere. We sense it in our spirit, and we are set to obey. Then we pray for the open doors and God will open them. Too often Christians approach it backwards. They say, *"God, if the door is open, then I will go do it."* God does not want us relying upon open doors for guidance because Satan can open doors too. The enemy of our souls can send along the wrong person or provide the wrong opportunity. We must check things out in the spirit rather than naively assuming that everything is of God. The world has mocked Christians for being naive and swallowing everything without having

God's wisdom. We need to ask for God's wisdom in all circumstances.

James 1:5: "If any of you lack wisdom, let him ask of God, that giveth to all men liberally, and upbraideth not; and it shall be given him."

Overcoming Pressure

"For we wrestle ... against the rulers of the darkness" (Ephesians 6:12a). We are in a wrestling match. That means we are struggling against something in the spiritual realm. Maximum effort is exerted in a wrestling match. The opponents give their all as they try to pin down each other. The devil is trying to pin us down to keep us from serving God. He is bringing tribulation against us in the form of pressure. Let us apply pressure back! Let us apply Holy Spirit pressure against the devil's pressure.

Because we are in the world, we are going to have tribulation **(John 16:33)**. In the beginning however, God's plan was that we be free from pressure. The Garden of Eden was a place of perfect peace. God did not put any pressure on Adam and Eve; all they had to do was obey. Pressure came through Satan. When man fell, Satan became the god of this world. And now by simply being in the world, we experience tribulation. Man's failure to obey opened the door to a corrupted creation.

In His mercy, God made a way out from under the dominion of the god of this world. That way is the cross. Through the forgiveness of our sins and the empowerment of the Holy Spirit, we can overcome any pressure the enemy brings upon us. God has given us victory over everything, even death. No Christian needs to fear death; because our spirits will immediately be with the Lord, and at the return of Christ, we will receive our resurrected bodies.

Death, sickness, sin ... these are temporary things, and in Christ we have victory over them. The Word tells us not only how to gain victory over problems, but also how to avoid many of them in the first place. A lot of the tribulation that we experience would never even come our way if we would simply obey the Word. If we do not lie, cheat, or steal, we can steer clear of numerous problems. God's commandments are for our own good.

Some Christians act as though God is a killjoy who does not want them doing anything that is fun. The truth is, He made those commandments so we could be blessed upon the earth. If we keep them, we will be blessed; if we do not, we will come under the curse. To come under the curse would be our own fault, for God did not plan the curse for us. He made the blessing for us and for all of those in His kingdom.

Overcoming Through Serving Others
God wants to bless us. He wants us to walk in victory, joy and peace. Christians should be enjoying the most blessed marriages on earth. We have the power of the Holy Spirit and His biblical principles to guide us. What holds back a beautiful married life? Selfishness! *"It is all about I, me, mine ... if you do not do such-and-such for me, I will not do thus-and-thus for you."* Selfishness is the number one killer of marriages.

The solution to this problem is nothing less than the sacrificial love of Christ, which always strives to serve others and to bless them. If two people are of this mindset, it makes for a successful marriage. My ministry is to promote my husband, and his ministry is to do the same for me. If we all walked that way, none of us would lack anything. If we all served one another, none of us would lack anything. But if we live in greed and selfishness, we all end up losing.

What do we do when our hearts are set to serve people, but they despise us instead? Sad to say, we have all have been hated by certain ones whom we have loved. How does one handle, for example, a visit to an unsaved relative who is so convicted by the presence of a Christian that he relates with animosity because of his own condition? Here is what we can do. Before the encounter we should pray along these lines: *"Lord, give us Your love for this person. Let Your love prevail. Help us to bless this person in word and deed. We forgive them. We take authority over the work of the enemy. We bind you, Satan, from the conversation and from speaking your lies to this person. Lord, use us; let us be a gift of mercy today."* This spiritual preparation works. Visits that would otherwise have been disastrous have been made peaceful. During our conversation, the enemy was not able to speak a word. Later, the individual may have continued his slander against us, but in our presence he could not because Satan was bound.

Disasters hit when we go unprepared. If we are thinking, *"What is that person going to say today? I do not even want to be around them. Must I go through with this?"* If we think this way, then the battle is already lost. To win, we need to overcome evil with good **(Romans 12:21)**. We should take the humble position, that of serving the individual. *"Lord, how can I help this person today?"* To walk in the headship position, we first have to take the low position of servanthood, as God's servants.

Truth, Part of Our Armor

Sometimes, Christians may become upset with governmental authorities, whether it be a judge, policeman, agency, or president. Our battle is not with officials simply doing their job. Our battle is with powers of darkness. In a legal confrontation, we bind those powers as necessary and pray, *"Lord, let Your truth prevail. If there is anything wrong on my part in this matter, show me. Judge this situation fairly, Lord. If it is against me, help me to cheerfully accept that and see where I have failed."* With this attitude of self-examination, we will win even if it looks like we lose. Whatever loss we incur in the natural, the Lord will make up to us, as long as we have the right heart attitude. With God on our side, we will never lose.

Ephesians 6:13 says, **"Wherefore take unto you the whole armour of God, that ye may be able to withstand in the evil day, and having done all, to stand."** Some Christians are no longer standing. They have been knocked out by the devil because they did not know how to prevail in warfare.

We prevail by putting on the whole armor of God. As **Ephesians 6** lists that armor, it first mentions the importance of truth: **"... having your loins girt about with truth ..."** **(Ephesians 6:14). 1 Peter 1:13a** tells us, **"... gird up the loins of your mind ..."** What does it mean to *"gird up the loins?"* It means we put the truth in our minds; we put on truth even when it confronts a lie within ourselves. We want any lie that we believe to be exposed. We Christians would get along much better if we were all willing to lay down any error we have believed. Maybe for thirty years we have misinterpreted a Scripture. Let us not react in pride and refuse to admit our mistake. Let us instead say, *"Lord, show me where I have been wrong and help me to admit it."*

As we put truth in our minds, we will respond with His truth whenever we are under pressure. Too many Christians are filling their minds with everything but the Word of God. They are filling themselves with content from secular magazines, hours of TV indulgence and the neighborhood gossip. Under pressure, they will come up with the world's reactions, rather than God's responses or the world's solutions rather than God's solutions. They will divorce just like the celebrity couple did, instead of praying their marriage through to victory as God would have them do.

Pressure Reveals What is in Us

What we put within us is what will come out of us in our day of trial. Our response under pressure will reveal our maturity, or lack of it, as Christians. Anyone can act like a victorious Christian on Sunday morning, praising God and all smiles. But what about at home? How quickly will we be provoked there? What do we still need to be cleansed of? The other day, I realized my need for a deeper work. It was one of those little irritating things that reveal bigger things in us. All I did was trip over my husband's bootjack that he had left out of place. I felt anger: *Why did he not put this away? Every time it is left out, I trip over it."* At least upon tripping I did say, *"Thank You, Jesus,"* but my heart was not in it. That is progress, though, from how I would have reacted years ago when I was in the world. God changes us and then continues to bring deeper changes. I had to confess, *"Lord, there is a work that still needs to be done in my heart. Remove any anger and let me always have a gentle spirit."*

It is tempting to blame others for our reactions. It would have been wonderful to have been able to blame my husband for my anger. We like to do that. Shifting the blame started, of course, with Adam and Eve. Adam blamed Eve and Eve blamed the devil. *"The devil made me do it,"* some say. Yet, the truth is that we have authority over the enemy. He cannot make us do anything as Christians, unless we give him consent. We have to agree with him.

So then, our Christian maturity is revealed by how we behave in everyday life, particularly under pressure. How do we act while driving the car or shopping at the grocery store? As businessmen, do we pad the expense account? How do we act in the "little things?" Are we honest in all financial matters? How do we treat other people? That is where the real Christ is evidenced in our lives. What do we do in our homes away from the church? It is not how we act in the church building that counts so much; anyone can act nicely there. We sometimes forget that God is not only at church, He is everywhere.

The Breastplate of Righteousness

Continuing with our spiritual armor, we are told to have on the breastplate of righteousness **(Ephesians 6:14)**. First, we must understand that there is none righteous. **"… There is none righteous, no, not one" (Romans 3:10b)**. I am not righteous, and you are not righteous. Yet there is one righteous – Jesus! Because of Him, we are righteous: His shed blood has made us so. The word righteous means to be in right standing with God. Jesus has made us to be in right standing with God. That means we can come boldly before His throne of grace.

We can come boldly before Him even if five minutes earlier we failed, such as my failure when I tripped over the bootjack by reacting in anger. If I did not know I was righteous in Christ, the devil would whisper, *"You cannot ask God for anything; you just failed Him."* The truth is **"If we confess our sins, he is faithful and just to forgive us our sins, and to cleanse us from all unrighteousness" (1 John 1:9)**. Therefore, upon confessing our sins, we are righteous and therefore have a right to receive what is ours through the righteousness of Christ.

Many Christians miss this truth. Maybe they have failed God, and asked Him for forgiveness, but never forgiven themselves. Along comes Satan with His condemnation and remembrance of their sin, keeping them from victory. But upon our confession, God says that He no longer remembers our sins! **"As far as the east is from the west, so far hath he removed our transgressions from us" (Psalm 103:12).** We need to know that we are righteous in Christ if we are ever going to prevail over Satan. I know who I am in Betty - *nothing!* I am nothing and I have nothing. I have nothing to teach. I cannot bless anyone. Anything that blesses you through this word is because of the Holy Spirit. Any good thing in me is because of the Holy Spirit, not because of Betty. I know Betty; she is nothing. Remember, Jesus said to call no man good, but God only **(Matthew 19:17)**.

Many people get the revelation of who they are, nothing, but then stop at that point. They see the filth of their own lives. They see themselves and the world as they are. It appears so hopeless that they cannot stand it, and some even kill themselves. The first step is a revelation of our own nothingness, but that must be followed with a revelation of who we are in Christ, and who Christ is in us.

In Christ, we are righteous. In Christ, we have victory and authority. In Christ, we can be as bold as lions. In Christ, there is neither male nor female. Therefore, a woman has the male authority of Christ in her life and can thereby stand against the devil. Black or white, young or old, male or female, Jew or Gentile, Christ is the answer for all. Christ in us, the name of Jesus; that is what causes the devil to flee.

If I come forward to minister without wearing the armor of God, I am defenseless. But if I walk forward with my armor on, the devil sees Christ and trembles. He does not tremble at me; he trembles at Christ coming forth from me. I have yielded to God and donned my armor; therefore, the enemy trembles and flees according to the verse below:

James 4:7: "Submit yourselves therefore to God. Resist the devil, and he will flee from you."

That armor includes the breastplate of righteousness. Wearing it, we can come boldly into the holy of holies. No matter what we have done, God does not condemn us because we have asked for forgiveness and cleansing. God sees our breastplate of righteousness.

Putting on Shoes of Peace

Next in our armor, we put shoes on our feet. **"And your feet shod with the preparation of the gospel of peace" (Ephesians 6:15).** This has two meanings. First, as children of God, we are to be peacemakers **(Matthew 5:9)**. If we are in strife with someone, we will not be victorious against the devil. To receive from God, we are going to have to walk in peace toward everyone - in a continual state of forgiveness and love. Maybe they have not made up with us yet, but as long as we have forgiven them and have asked them from our heart to forgive us, we will be free from strife. We are armed with the gospel of peace.

Secondly, we are to take the gospel of peace to others. We should be ready at all times to share what God has given us: reconciliation to Him through Christ. That is the gospel of peace: God is not mad at us anymore. His anger has been appeased through the blood of Jesus. God is angry at sin, but we have given our sins to Him and are cleansed by the blood of Christ. That is the good news we ought to be sharing with others. We ought to be telling them God loves them and that He has made a way for them to be free from their sins. We need to tell them that God will wash them clean in Christ. We need to be prepared, ready at any moment to share the gospel of peace, never backing away from the truth that makes men free.

Take the Shield of Faith

In donning our armor, we are told, **"Above all, taking the shield of faith ..." (Ephesians 6:16a).** Above all, faith is the most important piece of our armor. In fact, **"... whatsoever is not of faith is sin" (Romans 14:23b).** Faith is so crucial that besides being part of the armor, it is listed as both a gift and fruit of the Spirit. That is why we emphasize faith, and why faith teachings have been spread throughout the land. Yes, there have been abuses and extremes in the faith teachings, but that is the case with any truth of God. It does not nullify our responsibility to walk in faith.

In learning to walk in faith and believe for something from God, sometimes we have to start at the level we are on. Many Christians start by believing for a physical thing. That is fine. After we have exercised it there, we can believe for spiritual things - for souls to be saved. I have used faith in every realm, from physical to spiritual. It is by faith that we are going to overcome. Our faith will deliver our children. Our faith will bring financial releases. Our faith will end Satanic pressures. Our faith will bring us through anything.

Raise the shield of faith. Why? Because by it we will **"... be able to quench all the fiery darts of the wicked" (Ephesians 6:16b).** No matter what fiery dart the devil releases; no matter what he means to destroy us with, faith will stop his attack. We are not immune from his attacks, but as we raise the shield of faith, we will end them.

In the parable of the two houses **(Matthew 7:24-27),** one was built on sand and the other on rock. When the storms raged, only the house on the rock (Jesus and His Word) stood. Note that the storms of life came against both houses. We are not exempt from trouble, but we are exempt from what the enemy could make of that trouble. We have victory over what it could otherwise produce. By raising the shield of faith, we quench the fiery darts that would otherwise bring destruction.

The Helmet of Salvation

Our next piece of armor is the helmet of salvation **(Ephesians 6:17)**. We are to cover our minds, to protect them from that which would damage our spirits. **Proverbs 4:23** tells us, **"Keep thy heart with all diligence; for out of it are the issues of life."** We must guard our minds because the mind is the channel to the heart. We need to guard our minds against the thinking of the world and all of the devil's garbage.

Guard your children from the devil's music. Do not let them listen to ungodly music that conveys a spirit of witchcraft and rebellion against their spirits. No wonder so many teenagers are committing suicide. Another tool the enemy uses against our children is video games. Pass by a video arcade or look at some of the games on their cell phones and if you have spiritual discernment, you can see the snakes crawling in there. Then we wonder why our children are behaving strangely. They are picking up things in the spirit realm because they are not wearing the helmet of salvation to protect their minds.

If I am in a public place where demonic music is being played, I say, *"Lord, I have got on the helmet of salvation so that music will not enter my spirit."* With that barrier, I am not bothered, but without it, I start getting nervous. That is especially true for those who are rarely around such music. On the other hand, those who are openly exposing themselves to it can be oppressed by demons that thrive on it. If we work in such a place, we can pray for the Lord to change the music menu. We can also pray that restaurants where we eat will change their music. This can occur by the salvation of the owners.

We should be careful to guard our "ear gate" and our "eye gate" so unclean things do not enter in. A recently executed serial killer of many women admitted that pornography played a major role in corrupting his soul. Stand against this evil and ask for deliverance if it has touched your life.

As responsible parents, we must guard what our children hear and see. Many parents choose to place their offspring in Christian schools because so much of what children receive in public schools does not line up with God's Word. The pervasive secular humanism there instigates rebellion against parental authority. So then, we not only need to guard our own minds, but also our children's minds by not allowing them to access things on TV, computers and cell phones that are evil. Children should not be allowed to listen to demon inspired music nor play evil video games.

The Sword for Offensive Battle

Listed last is the one offensive weapon: the sword of the Spirit, which is God's Word. Defensive weapons such as the shield of faith keep the enemy from entering in, but to take territory from him, we need an offensive weapon. We need to use the sword of the Word of God.

Christ said that the gates of hell would not prevail against His church. Within the gates of hell are fenced-off prisoners: the unsaved, those bound up in sickness, rebellion and bitterness. Gates are stationary and immobile. We have to attack those gates with the sword of the Spirit. Here is our assault: *"In Jesus' name, I command you, Satan, to release the prisoners. God's Word promises that the seed of the righteous shall be delivered; therefore, you cannot keep my child in bondage. The Word says those of the covenant are under the blessing, not the curse, so remove your sickness from this person."* By the promises of God, by His Word, we war against the enemy. God will honor our covenant position as we battle for our children and grandchildren.

For too long, the church has been on the defensive, hiding behind the shield of faith. We have been crying out defensively for God to protect us, but God wants us to step out from our place of only hiding behind His shield. He wants us to raise high those shields of faith, wield our swords and move forward, steadily making progress against the enemy. We need to come against the enemy and bind his attempts to prevent churches from fulfilling what God has called them to do. We should take authority over spirits of division. We are called to spoil the enemy's territory and to demand that we be released from his deception. This aggression against the enemy, this warring by the Word of God, is what spiritual warfare is all about.

Some may feel that our warfare is too bold, too loud. But war is noisy. Bombs are dropping. The Words of God from our mouths are like spiritual missiles. We are releasing missiles into the enemy's territory. We are breaking through into his territory and releasing prisoners, those sick and in bondage. We are obtaining provisions to do the work of God; whatever may be needed. Every time I have been under satanic assault, my victory has come by warring in the spirit. Using spiritual tools has brought victory. Those tools include prayer. **"Praying always with all prayer and supplication in the Spirit, and watching thereunto with all perseverance and supplication for all saints" (Ephesians 6:18).** When I pray fervently in tongues and in the natural with all supplication, the enemy has to back off. Time and time again, I have seen this work.

Let us stand up in God's army with every piece of armor in place. Let us raise our shields of faith, wield our swords by speaking the Word of God over situations and gain victories for God. We are destined to be overcomers. In humility and God's power, let us begin to act like it!

In conclusion of this chapter, let us review *The Armor of God* by reading the scripture in the Amplified Bible.

Ephesians 6:10-18 (Amp):
10 In conclusion, be strong in the Lord [be empowered through your union with Him]; draw your strength from Him [that strength which His boundless might provides].

11 Put on God's whole armor [the armor of a heavy-armed soldier which God supplies], that you may be able successfully to stand up against [all] the strategies {and} the deceits of the devil.

12 For we are not wrestling with flesh and blood [contending only with physical opponents], but against the despotisms, against the powers, against [the master spirits who are] the world rulers of this present darkness, against the spirit forces of wickedness in the heavenly (supernatural) sphere.

13 Therefore put on God's complete armor, that you may be able to resist {and} stand your ground on the evil day [of danger], and, having done all [the crisis demands], to stand [firmly in your place].

14 Stand therefore [hold your ground], having tightened the belt of truth around your loins and having put on the breastplate of integrity {and} of moral rectitude {and} right standing with God,

15 And having shod your feet in preparation [to face the enemy with the firm-footed stability, the promptness, and the readiness produced by the good news] of the Gospel of peace.

16 Lift up over all the [covering] shield of saving faith, upon which you can quench all the flaming missiles of the wicked [one].

17 And take the helmet of salvation and the sword that the Spirit wields, which is the Word of God.

18 Pray at all times (on every occasion, in every season) in the Spirit, with all [manner of] prayer and entreaty. To that end keep alert and watch with strong purpose {and} perseverance, interceding in behalf of all the saints (God's consecrated people).

PERSONAL SPIRITUAL WARFARE

Chapter 5
The Promise of Victory

Overcoming Persecution

As we engage in spiritual warfare, we will face persecution and tribulation. Therefore, we need to keep the promise of victory before us. We cannot allow obstacles to discourage us. Jesus told us, **"These things I have spoken unto you, that in me ye might have peace. In the world ye shall have tribulation: but be of good cheer; I have overcome the world" (John 16:33).**

Revelation 12: 3-5 gives us a picture of the church's battle against Satan: **"And there appeared another wonder in heaven; and behold a great red dragon, having seven heads and ten horns, and seven crowns upon his heads. And his tail drew the third part of the stars of heaven, and did cast them to the earth: and the dragon stood before the woman which was ready to be delivered, for to devour her child as soon as it was born. And she brought forth a man child, who was to rule all nations with a rod of iron: and her child was caught up unto God, and to his throne."**

The book of **Revelation** is full of symbolic language. The "man child" speaks of the Lord Jesus Christ in His coming to the earth, His ruling over all, and His being caught up to the throne of God. The "woman" refers to Israel from which Jesus came forth; and yet the "woman" is also symbolic of the Church.

"And the woman fled into the wilderness, where she hath a place prepared of God, that they should feed her there a thousand two hundred and threescore days. And there

was war in heaven: Michael and his angels fought against the dragon; and the dragon fought and his angels, And prevailed not; neither was their place found any more in heaven. And the great dragon was cast out, that old serpent, called the Devil, and Satan, which deceiveth the whole world: he was cast out into the earth, and his angels were cast out with him" (Revelation 12:6-9).

As we noted in an earlier chapter, these fallen angels are now demonic spirits. "And I heard a loud voice saying in heaven, Now is come salvation, and strength, and the kingdom of our God, and the power of his Christ: for the accuser of our brethren is cast down, which accused them before our God day and night" (Revelation 12:10). If we are criticizing and accusing our brethren, we have fallen into the trap of the enemy, the original accuser.

"Therefore rejoice, ye heavens, and ye that dwell in them. Woe to the inhabiters of the earth and of the sea! for the devil is come down unto you, having great wrath, because he knoweth that he hath but a short time. And when the dragon saw that he was cast unto the earth, he persecuted the woman which brought forth the man child" (Revelation 12:12-13). Israel came under persecution, but this also refers to Satan's persecution of the church.

"And to the woman were given two wings of a great eagle, that she might fly into the wilderness, into her place, where she is nourished for a time, and times, and half a time, from the face of the serpent. And the serpent cast out of his mouth water as a flood after the woman, that he might cause her to be carried away of the flood. And the earth helped the woman, and the earth opened her mouth, and swallowed up the flood which the dragon cast out of his mouth. And the dragon was wroth with the woman, and went to make war with the remnant of her

seed, which keep the commandments of God, and have the testimony of Jesus Christ" (Revelation 12:14-17).

Satan is angry with the woman, God's people on the earth. He comes against the church with great wrath, knowing he has but a short time. We are in a battle against Satan because he hates all who represent Christ. Because of what Christ has done for you and me; Satan's anger is directed toward us.

The enemy delights in defiling Christians. He loves to get them to turn away; he loves to destroy their testimony and their faith. Satan's objective is to totally defeat those who keep the commandments of God and have the testimony of Jesus.

Our Legal Inheritance

The Scriptures reveal, however, that we are not to be destroyed by the wicked one, instead we have the victory over him through our Lord Jesus. Christ defeated Satan at the cross, and His victory is legally ours. But to walk in that victory, we have to understand it and use our spiritual tools. If we do not, we will be as defeated as those in the world. Many Christians constantly come under Satan's heel because they do not know how to war.

What does it mean to have the victory *legally?* Through Christ's sacrifice on the cross 2,000 years ago, mankind is *legally* saved. When Jesus cried, "It is finished," He meant the price had been paid for all men to be restored and elevated back to the original position Adam had lost. But not all receive that salvation because they will not confess their sins and by faith accept Christ. *Legally* everyone is healed. Christ took our infirmities. But like everything else in Christ, we have to appropriate it.

If we receive an inheritance legally, it is ours to enjoy. But if the will is not executed, the inheritance will be worthless to us. We will not receive a dime unless we appropriate it. We Christians must appropriate our inheritance. It is legally available, but we must walk in it. It is not an automatic thing.

Because Christians have not understood or walked in their inheritance, and have not exercised their authority over Satan, the church as a whole has not been victorious. However, Christ is returning for a Bride without spot or blemish **(Ephesians 5:27)**. He is returning for a glorious, holy church, a church walking in power over sin.

Power over sin is where we need to start in our own lives. We will never lead others to victory until we have victory ourselves **(Matthew 7:3-5)**. If we cannot rule and reign in our own personal lives, how are we ever going to rule and reign on earth with Him? Let us begin with the realization that sin no longer has power over us. **"Giving thanks unto the Father, which hath made us meet to be partakers of the inheritance of the saints in light: Who hath delivered us from the power of darkness, and hath translated us into the kingdom of his dear Son" (Colossians 1:12-13).** We have been delivered from the power of darkness and sin. Now we are in the light.

Walking free from the power of sin is dependent, of course, upon our 100% commitment to God. Anything less and we can forget about full victory, because we will constantly be harassed by Satan. In fact, we can be Christians yet still be serving Satan at times. **Romans 6:16** says, **"Know ye not, that to whom ye yield yourselves servants to obey, his servants ye are to whom ye obey; whether of sin unto death, or of obedience unto righteousness?"**

Authority in Christ

Now that we are in God's kingdom, the kingdom of light, we can walk free from that which entangles us in the world. God wants us to walk in this victory, not only for our own good, but also so that we can free others. God gives us authority so that we can see others saved, healed and delivered. Our authority is not so we can spout off that we are "King's Kids" and act like spoiled brats. Such an attitude reflects a lack of commitment.

It is a humbling experience to understand and begin to walk in the authority that God has given to us: *"Dear Lord, You mean You actually did this for us? That we can truly walk in this place?"* To me, it is the most amazing thing! We need to be grateful that God has given us this place to walk.

Note **Luke 10:17-19: "And the seventy returned again with joy, saying, Lord, even the devils are subject unto us through thy name. And he said unto them, I beheld Satan as lightning fall from heaven. Behold, I give unto you power to tread on serpents and scorpions, and over all the power of the enemy: and nothing shall by any means hurt you."** This power over the enemy was not restricted to the 70 disciples. It is available for any disciple of Christ; after all, He is the same yesterday, today, and forever **(Hebrews 13:8)**. We have the power to tread on serpents and scorpions. **Revelation 12:9** calls Satan **"... that old serpent ..."** He is under our feet. We have authority over him and anything he produces. Nothing shall harm us by any means.

The problem in the church is deception. Because we have not known our position in Christ, the devil has been walking all over us - instead of the other way around! Many Christians say, *"What a terrible week I have been having; the devil has really been after me."* The devil should be

running from us! We should be giving him a terrible week!
Every time he raises his ugly head, we should rise up in the
name and power of Jesus and send him running.

**"Notwithstanding in this rejoice not, that the spirits are
subject unto you; but rather rejoice, because your names
are written in heaven" (Luke 10:20).** We should not
become prideful about our authority in Christ. It is a cause
for gratitude, of course, but our chief cause for rejoicing is
our salvation and eternal life.

Give the Enemy No Place

As long as we are walking in God's will, the devil can't hurt
us. **"Behold, I give unto you power to tread on serpents
and scorpions, and over all the power of the enemy: and
nothing shall by any means hurt you." (Luke 10:19).** On
the other hand, if we get outside of His will, we lose our
protection. We become easy prey for the enemy who
delights in destroying God's people. Satan is constantly
looking for ways to get us out of God's will. He tries to
deceive us into agreeing with him.

Remember, there are three ways Satan takes advantage of
people: *ignorance, deception* and *rebellion. Ignorance* of
God's Word means that people are not aware of their
inheritance and authority, *deception* causes people to think
that they are doing God's will when they are not, and
rebellion finds people willfully walking the opposite
direction from God. All three lead to defeat. **1 John 3:8**
tells us, **"He that committeth sin is of the devil; for the
devil sinneth from the beginning. For this purpose the
Son of God was manifested, that he might destroy the
works of the devil."**

Christ came to do away with Satan's works. He came to do
away with man's sin problem. When we sin, the works of

Satan come forth. Sin produces the devil's works, whereas obedience to God brings blessing. We are either doing the works of God by obeying Him, or we are doing the works of the devil.

As Christians drift away from God's will, the works of the devil show up in their marriages, their children, their finances, and their whole lives. We have all experienced battles in these areas. Satan tries the same old things with all Christians. He is out to destroy churches, marriages, families, health - everything. But overcoming Christians maintain their victory because they know their rights in Christ Jesus. Those who have not discovered the way to victory in Jesus, fall prey to the enemy and lose everything.

Overcoming in Trials

Some Christians go through a trial, whereas others are under a trial. Those going *through* have peace and victory in the midst of it all. They will say, *"We are experiencing some problems but, praise God, we have got peace. God is on the throne, and He is working things out."* Such Christians continue to walk in love and joy and faith no matter what kind of trial they are experiencing. But Christians who are under a trial, those who let the trial get them down, will become fearful. They are worried, anxious, without hope, not knowing what to do next. They are heading for defeat because they have never put on the whole armor of God. They have not fought for His victory; nor asked for His faith, peace and joy in the midst of the trial. Those who are walking in joy and faith during their trials will end up victorious; and those who are walking without hope will end up defeated.

All things *do not* work together for good for everyone. They work for good for **"… them that love God, to them that are called according to his purpose" (Romans 8:28b).**

Those who are totally surrendered to God can claim this promise of everything working for good in their lives. No matter what the enemy brings against us, God will turn it to good, if we are completely His. But if we do not love Him; if we are not surrendered, then the enemy's assault will work harm in our lives. Some become angry at God when things go wrong; but God does not bring bad things into our lives - the devil does.

In the great commission, Christ said, **"... Go ye into all the world, and preach the gospel to every creature. He that believeth and is baptized shall be saved; but he that believeth not shall be damned. And these signs shall follow them that believe; In my name shall they cast out devils; they shall speak with new tongues; They shall take up serpents; and if they drink any deadly thing, it shall not hurt them; they shall lay hands on the sick, and they shall recover" (Mark 16:15b-18).**

This commission was given to all believers; not just to the first - century disciples. Christ said to go into all the world, so obviously His words are yet for the church today. As some go forth, however, they are only preaching a portion of the gospel. They are sharing the message of salvation but stopping there. The full gospel message includes casting out devils, speaking in tongues, healing the sick, walking in authority over Satan and his powers and being immune from harm.

That certainly does not sound like an inadequate church! It is a church full of the power of God. It is a church with the power to cast out devils, speak in tongues and heal the sick. **"They shall take up serpents ..." (Mark 16:18a).** Who are the serpents? Satan and his demons, of course! The church has power over these foes.

The Apostle Paul had an encounter with an actual serpent. On the island of Melita, a viper latched onto his hand, but Paul simply shook off the beast into the fire **(Acts 28:5)**. Those observing were astonished when Paul suffered no harm from the venom. They thought that he was a god, but Paul knew it was the power of Jesus' name that gave him authority over serpents, even in the natural realm. This does not mean we should be handling vipers as proof of our faith. "Take up serpents" has a spiritual emphasis. It refers to our power over the wicked one.

Exercising Our Authority
"So then after the Lord had spoken unto them, he was received up into heaven, and sat on the right hand of God. And they went forth, and preached everywhere, the Lord working with them, and confirming the word with signs following. Amen" (Mark 16:19-20).

The true church of God is going to have signs following; signs that confirm the word and prove that God's power dwells within. Note that it is the "Lord working *with* them." He is not working outside of us. We have a part to play in what God is doing in the earth. We are to do our part, and God will do His. Our part is obedience, and as we obey Him, He supplies the power, the signs and wonders, the miracles; all the things we cannot do. We do the possible and He does the impossible. That is what faith is all about: we move in obedience to His Word and, as we do, God's power is made manifest and signs follow.

Christ said**, "These things I have spoken unto you, that in me ye might have peace. In the world ye shall have tribulation: but be of good cheer; I have overcome the world" (John 16:33).** As we have pointed out earlier, we are going to encounter battles. But we are to be of good cheer since Christ has overcome them and through Him, we also can overcome. When we see the enemy trying to come against us, it should be a cause for rejoicing because it is an opportunity for the Lord to show Himself as mighty! For instance, if the enemy should try to disrupt a church service, we should be of good cheer as we take authority over the enemy: *"We bind you, Satan, in Jesus' name. We take authority over your disturbance. You will not speak here today. God is in charge of this service."* As we move in our authority, we will see God accomplish His work, rather than the enemy. We can do this ahead of time in intercessory prayer, so we rarely have a public service disturbed.

It is the same in our homes. As Christians, we have authority there. If our children are unruly and disobedient, we can take spiritual authority over that rebellion, as well as exercise our authority in the natural realm. **"He that spareth his rod hateth his son: but he that loveth him chasteneth him betimes" (Proverbs 13:24).** Scriptural discipline teaches children to obey. Of course, we are not talking about child abuse. We are *not* talking about striking children with injurious objects! We are *not* to discipline them in anger, or in an out-of-control manner. But a proper paddling to their little bottoms works. Spanking may be in order but let us also be sure that we are taking authority in our prayer closets. Tormenting, demonic powers may be coming against our children. We have to pray against any spirits the enemy would use against them.

What about a child who erupts into a rage and beats his head against the floor? He is suffering under demonic assault. If we cast out the demon, the child will be free from such behavior. There are children who scream at night because a tormenting spirit assaults them. If we take authority over such spirits, the children will sleep in peace. Too often, parents are not aware of the spiritual causes behind their children's problems. They may think, *"Well, it is just part of life,"* and thereby allow the enemy to get away with his evil works. It may be a part of this life, but what happens in the natural world has spiritual causes. **Proverbs 26:2b** says, **"... the curse causeless shall not come."** Whatever torments a child is from the devil, and we need to exercise our authority over him.

Discernment is Needed

How can we tell whether our children's problems need to be dealt with primarily in the spirit or in the natural? God has given us spiritual discernment. As we pray, He will show us what may be causing the problems. Then, we will know what to do, whether it is praying against demonic assault or administering discipline in the natural. As sons of God, we live on a higher level, a spiritual level, so we are to discern how to properly deal with problems.

Entrepreneurs may experience business problems because of demonic assault. If so, they should deal with it on a spiritual level and bind up the powers of darkness. For example, a spirit of division could hit their employees. In that case, they should pray against that attack. On the other hand, they may have a business problem that calls for an answer in the natural. Through prayer, they can know what is behind any problem and how to deal with it.

We all need to pray to find God's leading. We have to walk in the Spirit; otherwise, we will not know what to do. People stay in confusion, uncertain of the direction they are to take, until they pray, *"Lord, show me what is wrong. Show me what I need to do to make corrections in my life, my marriage, my business."* God will then lead with the answers that are sometimes spiritual answers, or sometimes natural answers, or sometimes, both.

When the problems are spiritual, involving powers of darkness, the only way to deal with them is on a spiritual level, taking authority over them and casting evil spirits out. We cannot reason or plead with those under demonic influence. That will not change them. Instead, we have to deal with the underlying spirits. Too often, as Christians we have failed to understand this, so the enemy's work has gone undetected and unhindered.

People will avoid dealing with evil spirits. They may say, *"Do not talk about the devil - that gives him glory."* Nonsense! We are not giving him glory; we are exposing him so he can be dealt with! Only then can we walk in victory.

There are two extremes to avoid when talking about Satan. The first is not to mention him at all. But the Bible does not tell us to *ignore* the enemy, and he will go away; rather, it says to *resist* him and he will flee **(James 4:7)**. To resist him, we have got to know where he is hiding and how to deal with him. Yet, some Christians refuse to deal with him. Their attitude is, *"Praise God; I love God, so everything is going to be all right."* They might love God, but everything is not all right; the enemy is defeating them in situation after situation.

The other extreme is that of seeing a demon behind every rock, bush and tree in sight. Christians can become so "demon conscious" that they lose their awareness of the Lord. Their minds are on a constant devil hunt, rather than on Jesus. Sure, there are plenty of demons around, but our task is not always to be discerning them. For instance, when I am grocery shopping, I am not spending that time discerning spirits in the other shoppers; I am simply buying groceries. On the other hand, I am available if God wants to use me. If He prompts me to discern something or pray for someone, I am ready for that.

If we keep our focus on the Lord, it is not unusual to encounter situations that call for our prayers. Once as my late husband Bud and I stepped out of a taxi, we heard two men nearby shouting at each other. Moments later they were exchanging blows. Bud and I quickly prayed against the devil and the anger. We loosed God's peace into the situation. Immediately the men calmed down. We need to use our authority when we come upon an out-of-control situation.

Led by the Spirit

I have come upon accident scenes and prayed for the injured as God has led. Once at an auto crash scene, I went into deep travail. God especially wanted prayer for that situation as I felt compelled to pray and pray, even though I knew none of the involved parties. Other times God has not led me into such deep involvement, either physically or spiritually. I always add my prayer, but my level of involvement is determined by the leading of the Lord and what help has already been provided.

As we are attentive to the Spirit of the Lord, God will use us to somehow help in battles we come across. We are not where we are by luck or fate. We do not walk by fate; we walk by faith in the living God. We walk, believing that each day we will be productive in Christ, and do His will. Luck has nothing to do with our walk. It is God who protects and blesses us. Because we are a covenant people, we have His divine protection, and we are able to reach out and help others as well.

Note **1 Corinthians 15:57: "But thanks be to God, which giveth us the victory through our Lord Jesus Christ."**

Thanks be to God who does give us victory, not through ourselves but through Christ Jesus. Continuing with **verse 58**, **"Therefore, my beloved brethren, be ye stedfast, unmoveable, always abounding in the work of the Lord, forasmuch as ye know that your labour is not in vain in the Lord."** Let us be steadfast, immovable, standing solid in faith every day. Let us not be wishy-washy. That double-minded attitude is the surest route to defeat. Believing God one moment and doubting Him the next will never bring us to victory. Saying one moment that God has told us to do "such-and-such," and changing our minds the next moment will never produce growth.

Some Christians will approach a ministry and declare, *"God has led me to be a part of your church, to support you and to learn from you."* Two months later they leave. Did God really lead them or not? Typically, they run into a dedication problem. They refuse to discipline their flesh and grow in God. They state that God has told them to come, but then they leave. They are definitely missing God someplace, either in coming or going.

Some Christians will say God has shown them to pray daily with their family, or stop overspending, or start fasting. But they never do it. That is disobedience. And then they wonder why there is no victory in their lives.

We Must Conform to the Word of God
Problems arise when we do not conform to the Word of God. In marriage counseling, the best advice we can give is for both individuals to conform to the Word. Typically, there is something wrong on both sides. We do not take sides. The only side is the Word of God. If the parties in strife conform to what the Word teaches, peace will reign in their marriage. Conforming to the Word brings love and unity. It is the only source of true unity.

112

There is plenty of false unity in the world. For example, the World Council of Churches has compromised much in their efforts to unite various religious groups. We cannot be in unity with everyone and everything. That has been a problem in America. In the name of freedom, we have allowed ungodly abominations to run unchecked, be it abortion or pornography or idolatrous eastern religions. According to God's Word, freedom carries responsibilities. Without responsibilities and an adherence to His standards, there is no true freedom. Only God's Word will set us free. **"And ye shall know the truth, and the truth shall make you free" (John 8:32).** No wonder America is experiencing great difficulties. The founding fathers' idea of freedom of religion meant freedom to serve the God of the Bible, not false gods. Freedom meant liberty to obey the Bible, not to flaunt behavior totally contrary to the Word such as homosexuality and witchcraft.

Confusion reigns when we stray from the standard of God's Word. But adherence to His Word will bring stability and true unity. God is the referee. He has the final say in all matters. We should be solving all of our problems, whether they are at home, in the church, or on the national level, through the Word of God. If we did this, it would bring peace and harmony, rather than the mess that the whole world is in. I praise God that with the soon return of Jesus, this world will be set in order. He will rule with a rod of iron. Under His authority, there will be peace and harmony. What a wonderful day that will be!

The truth is, we can walk in that day now on a personal level. We can rule and reign now in our personal lives. *Today* we can have peace and harmony. Note **Romans 8:35-37, "Who shall separate us from the love of Christ? shall tribulation, or distress, or persecution, or famine, or nakedness, or peril, or sword? As it is written, For thy** sake we are killed all the day long; we are accounted as sheep for the slaughter. Nay, in all these things we are more than conquerors through him that loved us."** <u>More</u> than conquerors! Through Christ we have victory over anything and everything that the enemy would try to bring against us. We only need to keep our eyes on Jesus and have full faith in Him.

God's Blessings Belong to Us
"What shall we then say to these things? If God be for us, who can be against us? He that spared not his own Son, but delivered him up for us all, how shall he not with him also freely give us all things?" (Romans 8:31-32). When God gave His Son for us, He gave that which was dearest to Him. The Word says that if He gave that which was most important to Him, "His Son," will He not also give us all things?

Of course, these things would only be those that are good for us. God wants to fulfill our righteous desires, in His way and in His time **(Psalm 37:4)**. Sometimes we want things ahead of God's timing, before we are ready for them. A premature blessing would only hurt us. In His wisdom, God blesses us when we are ready to handle them. If we have unrighteous desires, God wants to remove them from our hearts. All we have to do is pray, *"Lord, remove every unrighteous desire from my heart. Fill me with Your desires. Give me only those things that are of You. Thank You for the blessings that You have given to me. Thank You for what Jesus has done for me."*

God has done so much for us. He has given us salvation, healing, love, joy, peace, prosperity and on and on. Some Christians want to play the martyr role, refusing to enjoy any of God's blessings. They say they want to do without everything. Apart from God's leading, such an attitude can be carried to an extreme. Of course, there is a time for sacrifice. We need to be willing to sacrifice whenever the occasion demands. In fact, many Christians need to do more of that. Christians can become extremist either way, always enjoying their blessings in Christ, but never sacrificing anything, or never enjoying any of His blessings because they are acting like martyrs by refusing His blessings.

We are to enjoy His blessings. Christ died that they might be ours. Our God is a loving Father who wants to bless us with good things, just as long as those things are not the focus of our hearts. Those things cannot come between our Father and us. God can give us good things as long as we hold them loosely, willing to give them up at a moment's notice. But if we are clutching things to our hearts, they will end up being a hindrance to us. We must learn to surrender all at the altar.

Isaiah 54:17 says, **"No weapon that is formed against thee shall prosper; and every tongue that shall rise against thee in judgment thou shalt condemn. This is the heritage of the servants of the Lord, and their righteousness is of me, saith the Lord."** What a victory promise! No matter what weapon the enemy would form against us, we are assured of victory. Upon the enemy's assault, our immediate thoughts should be, *"Hallelujah, another opportunity for the Lord's victory."* We should be "victory conscious." There is no need for us to be beaten down by the devil.

In the Amplified Version of the Bible, it says **"... every tongue that rises against us to condemn us we shall prove to be wrong."** How shall we "prove wrong" the lying tongues? By our lives! As we walk in obedience to Christ, we will prove the accusations wrong. Our lives will be the proof that we were hearing the Lord and obeying His Word.

115

Receiving Our Inheritance

Another victory promise is found in **Revelation 21:7: "He that overcometh shall inherit all things; and I will be his God, and he shall be my son."** This verse speaks both of our inheritance and of our relationship. Our relationship to Him is of primary importance: He is to be our God, and we are to be His sons or daughters. Anything that comes between that relationship, even good things, will cause us to live beneath the place God would have us to be. No matter how good something is that God has given us, whether it is our marriage, family, home, or anything else, we cannot allow it to come between us and our relationship with the Lord.

God wants to give us good things. He has promised as much. Legally, the blessings belong to us. However, even though we might legally own something, there is the possibility that we might never use or enjoy it. A person may have a legal title to a car, but if he never drives it, he will not enjoy the benefits of ownership. If the car is stolen from him, he will still own it, but he will not be able to use it. The car owner not only needs a legal piece of paper proving ownership, but he also needs to get in the car and drive it, otherwise his ownership is useless.

So many Christians are like a car owner who never drives. We already have the legal piece of paper. We have inherited all things in Christ. But too many of us are not enjoying our inheritance. We are struggling along the freeway on foot when we could be driving. In fact, many have not even learned how to drive. They do not know how to appropriate their inheritance in Christ. They do not know how to appropriate His healing for their bodies or emotions; His joy for their marriages; His abundance in their finances; His final victory over recurring sins and bondages; and His power to bring deliverance to others and see souls saved.

Christ died that we might walk in these things. He died that we might have power in all these areas, including the power to witness to others of salvation in Him. He died that we might be able to walk away from earthly things; counting them as nothing, as we go forth in His service.

Without His love motivating us, we could never go forth in His service. When I was young in the Lord, I never wanted to serve in the mission field. But when I served in India, God gave me such a love for the people that I loved every minute of being there because the life of Christ within me came forth. He gave me love and strength and endurance. In my own strength, I never could have slept in a mud hut with a hungry rat in the same room. I prayed, *"Father, I confess my weakness here. Give me the power to sleep here in peace."* And He did. The next night, a cat showed up in the hut, and no one knew where it came from. Our loving Father had sent that cat to solve the rat and mice problem. That may seem minor to some, but when we face any situation, major or minor, God will give us power to overcome.

Perhaps we fear approaching a fellow Christian to remedy a wrong. If we ask Him, God will give us the power to do it. Maybe we need to confess something to our employer. God will give us the strength. He will enable us to face any situation, no matter how much we might dread it.

We have seen from God's Word that we are called to walk in victory; not defeat. We especially need that overcoming spirit in this hour of pessimism. We are surrounded by pessimism and tribulation. We do not need to wait for the great tribulation; we already have tribulation in our individual lives with extreme pressure from the enemy! But once again, remember Christ's words, **"These things I have spoken unto you, that in me ye might have peace. In the world ye shall have tribulation: but be of good cheer; I have overcome the world" (John 16:33).**

We are overcomers. May that truth be so real to our hearts. May we not receive it in pride, but in humility. Some would strut about in pride, declaring that they are just like Jesus. That is not the correct attitude for overcomers. We should be humbly thanking God for our overcoming position and then, walking in it, through the power of the Holy Spirit, we will be effective in changing this world. God wants to use us to see people saved, healed and delivered; and walking in victory rather than defeat.

PERSONAL SPIRITUAL WARFARE

Chapter 6
Our Tools for Battle

Prayer is God's Provision for War

As we engage in spiritual warfare, we need to use the tools God has made available. On the natural level, specific industries require specific tools. A carpenter, for example, cannot build a house without his saw and hammer. And we cannot be victorious without the use of our spiritual tools.

Our first tool in battling the enemy is prayer. **Ephesians 6:18** says, **"Praying always with all prayer and supplication in the Spirit, and watching thereunto with all perseverance and supplication for all saints."** Note that we are to pray *"with all prayer."* There are different types of prayer. Two major categories of prayer are praying in the natural and praying in the spirit.

"Praying in the spirit" means praying in tongues. Paul makes this clear: **"For he that speaketh in an unknown tongue speaketh not unto men, but unto God: for no man understandeth him; howbeit in the spirit he speaketh mysteries"** (1 Corinthians 14:2). A few verses later, Paul writes, **"I will pray with the spirit, and I will pray with the understanding also"** (1 Corinthians 14:15a). We are to pray both in "the natural" and in "the spirit."

Our praying is to be **"with all perseverance."** Let us persevere; not giving up when we do not see immediate answers. We live in an age when so much is "instant." In the area of food alone, we have instant coffee, instant soup, instant mashed potatoes, and so on. So, it is not surprising that we want instant answers when we pray. But God says to persevere.

Pray **"for all saints."** We are not to be selfish in our prayers, thinking only of our own needs. We are to pray for others in the body of Christ. We want to see their needs met.

"Pray without ceasing" (1 Thessalonians 5:17). Obviously, we cannot be in constant prayer in the traditional sense, with our eyes closed and mouth open. What does it mean to pray without ceasing? It means that at all times we are to be in an attitude of prayer. Our focus always needs to be on Him. That way, as a situation arises that calls for prayer, we are ready. We pray immediately. To pray without ceasing also means not to cease in our prayer life. We need to be faithful and consistent in taking time to pray.

Concerning prayer, Christ said, **"Ask, and it shall be given you; seek, and ye shall find; knock, and it shall be opened unto you: For every one that asketh receiveth; and he that seeketh findeth; and to him that knocketh it shall be opened" (Matthew 7:7-8).** We are to do three things: *ask, seek, knock.* If we do these things, we will obtain what we are believing for, not maybe, but for certain. Asking and seeking and knocking require persistence. It is not that God is trying to withhold from us, but rather the enemy is working to prevent us from receiving what God wants us to have. That is why God tells us to be persistent in our prayer.

Persistent Prayer

There are two extremes to avoid in prayer. The first is begging God, pleading with Him and asking the same thing over and over again with no expectation of an answer. Those who pray this way never receive the answer in their spirits and do not thank God that it is done. They do not receive because they do not truly believe that He will do it. They allow the devil to talk them out of it.

At the other extreme are those who pray once about something and then never pray about it again. They feel that because they have prayed once, that God is going to answer. Often, however, we have to keep praying over a matter, but not necessarily in the same way each time. Also, we can begin thanking God for the things we ask of Him.

Let us be balanced! We are lacking in faith if we repetitively ask but never receive. And we are moving in pride or ignorance if we are in the habit of only asking once, rather than battling through, praying in different ways about the situation, not rotely, asking the same thing over and over again, when we should be praising Him for the answers.

When I first begin praying for someone's salvation, I believe that God is going to save that person. But I do not stop after one prayer. As I battle for that soul, I will find myself praying different ways. Often, I will bind the enemy from blinding the person's eyes to his need for salvation in Christ. Or I may need to pray the person away from harmful involvement with the wrong individuals or something cultish or demonic. Or the needed prayer may be that the person receives a revelation of God's love and goodness. We just need to be guided by the Holy Spirit as to how we need to pray in different situations.

As I surround the person in prayer until salvation comes, I am not begging God. I am not saying over and over again, *"Oh God, save him; Oh God, save him."* Our prayers need to include thanksgiving that God is doing the work. *"Thank You, Lord, that You are working today to save that loved one. Thank You that You have accomplished it in the spirit and there is going to be the manifestation in the natural realm."* We need to thank God and receive it as being done. So then, when the Word says to "ask, seek and knock", it is not telling us to beg, beg and beg. Rather, it is telling us to ask with a deep expectancy. We should *expect* to receive!

Fervency is also an essential ingredient in prayer. **"... The effectual fervent prayer of a righteous man availeth much. Elias was a man subject to like passions as we are, and he prayed earnestly that it might not rain: and it rained not on the earth by the space of three years and six months. And he prayed again, and the heaven gave rain, and the earth brought forth her fruit" (James 5:16b-18).**

Effectual, fervent prayer makes things happen. No wonder the enemy sometimes brings heaviness or sleepiness to us when we enter into prayer. When he does, we need to forcibly rebuke him. There are times when we may need to take a quick nap and then pray some more when we wake up. That is better than just muttering along in our prayers without any fervency. A prayer that lacks fervency is not accomplishing much in the spirit realm. One advantage to praying in the morning is that we are more likely to be fervent when our bodies are refreshed. But when we pray late at night, the enemy may use our weariness against us.

Let us be involved in our prayers. Let us put our whole hearts into them. What if a visitor to your home sat there muttering and not really paying attention to the conversation? Would you be enthused about conversing with him? Prayer is a *conversation* with God. Enter into it with enthusiasm! And do not let it be one-sided. Let the Holy Spirit speak. Our prayer time should always include times of listening to the voice of the Lord as He speaks through His Spirit and His Word. After a time of prayer, open the Bible, read and study it, and God generally will speak from His Word. Sometimes Holy Spirit will bring a scripture to your mind with your needed answer.

The Tool of Agreement in Prayer

In prayer, there is great power in agreement. Christ said, **"Verily I say unto you, Whatsoever ye shall bind on earth shall be bound in heaven: and whatsoever ye shall loose on earth shall be loosed in heaven. Again I say unto you, That if two of you shall agree on earth as touching anything that they shall ask, it shall be done for them of my Father which is in heaven. For where two or three are gathered together in my name, there am I in the midst of them" (Matthew 18:18-20).** This is known as "the prayer of agreement." If we shall agree together in prayer, it shall be done.

Of course, this does not mean we can arbitrarily pick out just anything to agree on. We must choose the things that are God's will, things that line up with His Word. We should not be motivated by lust, deciding we want a huge house or a fancy car and then looking for someone to agree with us about such things. It is not that God will not give us material things when we have a need, but we must be certain that we are being motivated by His Spirit and not a spirit of lust. The prayer of agreement will work if the prayer burden lines up with God's Word and is what the Holy Spirit is speaking to us about.

When a husband and wife unite in prayer, great power is released. That is why the Scriptures admonish us to avoid strife with our spouses. Such strife will hinder our prayers according to **1 Peter 3:7: "Likewise, ye husbands, dwell with them according to knowledge, giving honour unto the wife, as unto the weaker vessel, and as being heirs together of the grace of life; that your prayers be not hindered."** For that matter, if we are angry with anyone, our prayers will be short-circuited.

In the Amplified Version of the Bible, **Matthew 18:18** says that whatever is *already* bound in heaven shall be bound on earth and that whatever is *already* loosed on earth shall be loosed in heaven. What does it mean by "already bound" and "already loosed?" It refers to what the Word of God has already promised. For example, the Word declares that **"... by whose stripes ye were healed" (1 Peter 2:24b).** It has already been loosed on earth. We can have a brother agree with us for healing and it shall be. The Word declares that our seed are blessed and shall be delivered **(Proverbs 11:21).** It has already been loosed on earth. We can agree with a fellow Christian that our children are delivered out of the hand of the enemy, and it shall be. Whatever God's Word has already loosed on earth is ours, as we enter into the prayer of agreement.

"... a threefold cord is not quickly broken" (Ecclesiastes 4:12b). If two Christians and the Holy Spirit are in agreement, a threefold cord is created. The enemy is bound by that strong cord and cannot prevent the prayer answer from coming through.

The Tool of Speaking the Word

Another essential tool is speaking the Word of God. **Ephesians 6:17b** refers to the Word as **"the sword of the Spirit."** It is the only offensive weapon listed in **Ephesians 6**, the chapter on the armor of God. It is by the Word that we take territory for God. Christ referred to the gates of hell **(Matthew 16:18b).** "Gates" are attached to a fence and a fence encircles territory. Using "the sword of the Spirit," we can crash through those gates of hell into enemy territory and take over. Whatever Satan has bound up in darkness we can loose into the kingdom of God. **"... the gates of hell shall not prevail against it"** (His church) **(Matthew 16:18b).**

Christ Himself used the Word in dealing with the devil **(Luke 4:1-13)**. Three times Satan tempted Him in the wilderness, and each time Christ responded, *"It is written."* Christ did not ignore the enemy. Instead, He fought Him off with "the sword of the Spirit." Note the first temptation: For forty days Christ had not eaten. **"... he afterward hungered. And the devil said unto him, If thou be the Son of God, command this stone that it be made bread. And Jesus answered him, saying, It is written, That man shall not live by bread alone, but by every word of God"** **(Luke 4:2b-4).**

Christ used "the Word" against the enemy. When we are tempted, let us likewise chase the enemy off with "the sword of the Spirit." Jesus quoted the Scripture that we are not to live by bread alone, but by every word of God. As we are filling our lives with His Word, living by it and agreeing with it, we can use God's Word against the enemy and he must flee.

In the second temptation against Christ, **"And the devil, taking him up into an high mountain, shewed unto him all the kingdoms of the world in a moment of time. And the devil said unto him, All this power will I give thee, and the glory of them: for that is delivered unto me; and to whomsoever I will I give it"** (Luke 4:5-6). Notice that the enemy claimed ownership of all the kingdoms of this world. He could not have offered Jesus something that was not his. How did Satan gain this earth?

Originally, God put Adam in charge; but when Adam fell to Satan's temptation, the control of the earth was relinquished to the Tempter. The good news is that due to Christ's sacrifice on the cross we have gained back the authority that Adam lost.

The earth no longer belongs to Satan, because Christ won the victory over him at the cross. The only reason Satan still hangs on to the earth is that most Christians have not exercised their authority over him through their inheritance in Christ. **"The earth is the Lord's, and the fulness thereof ..." (Psalm 24:1a).** This earth is *God's*, not Satan's.

God is moving in the earth, awakening His people to their position in Christ. He is prompting us to walk in our authority, so that the works of the devil might be destroyed. When tempted, Christ was able to use the Word against the enemy because the Scriptures lived in His heart. Likewise, we need to have the Word dwelling in us so that when we are tempted, we will automatically respond with the Word. For example, when we are tempted to passively lie down and accept sickness, we need to fight back with the Word. Whether or not we feel like it, we need to fight.

Christians fall into error when they follow their feelings rather than the Word of God. They may say they do not feel like God is with them. Yet, the Word promises, **"... I will never leave thee, nor forsake thee" (Hebrews 13:5b).** Sometimes, we have to receive His presence by faith, even when we do not sense it. In all areas, we need to go by the Word, not by our feelings. We may not feel like fellowshipping on a particular Sunday morning, but the Word says, **"Not forsaking the assembling of ourselves together ..." (Hebrews 10:25a).** Again, we should go by the Word, not our feelings.

God wants us to reach the place where all that we need is His Word. Our faith should not be dependent upon a sign or a manifestation or a confirmation. When the centurion came to Christ on behalf of his servant, the Lord volunteered to go to the sick one. But the centurion said, **"... speak the word only, and my servant shall be healed" (Matthew 8:8b).**

The Word alone brought healing to that servant. Let us walk on that same level of faith. Let us not require that God somehow prove that He is working on our prayers. The proof is the Word! The highest level of faith will stand on the Word of God and the Word of God alone. Our attitude should be *God said it; we believe it; and that settles it!*

The Tool of the Name of Jesus

We have been given so many tools to overcome the devil's attacks. One of our most powerful tools is "the name of Jesus." **"... Verily, verily, I say unto you, Whatsoever ye shall ask the Father in my name, he will give it you" (John 16:23b).** The proper approach to the Father is in "the name of Jesus." In that name, we will receive whatever we ask as long as our request lines up with His Word. He did not say He would withhold from us; on the contrary, He said He would give to those who ask.

Christ said, **"... In my name shall they cast out devils; they shall speak with new tongues; They shall take up serpents; and if they drink any deadly thing, it shall not hurt them; they shall lay hands on the sick, and they shall recover" (Mark 16:17b-18).**

He said, **"In my name."** We will not accomplish anything apart from His name. Demons will not respond to your name or mine, but they will submit to the name of Jesus. In confronting demons, we must always be sure to use the mighty name of Jesus.

One of the most effective ways to pray is to pray the Word of God. As we open the Bible and pray appropriate Scriptures over people and circumstances, God's Word will come to pass.

Let us combine these prayer tools. Let us speak the Word in prayer, use the name of Jesus, stand on the Word alone, agree with others in prayer, pray fervently and with persistence, without ceasing, in the natural and in the spirit. Using all of our prayer tools will make us effective prayer warriors.

Praise, Another Tool

Praise is another tool God has given us. As a carpenter builds a house, he does not use only one type of tool. He may use a variety of saws for a while, but then there comes a time for the hammer. Likewise, we sometimes have to change tools for different jobs. We may have to switch from various ways of praying and begin praising. There are occasions when praise will run the devil off faster than anything else.

"Rejoice evermore ... In everything give thanks: for this is the will of God in Christ Jesus concerning you" (1 Thessalonians 5:16,18). We are commanded to rejoice; to be full of praise and thanksgiving.

Incidentally, when we are told to give thanks in everything, it does not mean that the negative things that occur are from God. They are not. We are not to praise God *for* all things, but rather *in* all things. For instance, we do not thank God for sickness, it is not from Him; but we do maintain our thankful attitude in the midst of it. We can say, *"Lord, I praise You that You are greater than this assault from the enemy. I thank You for the victory. I love You no matter what I am going through."* The devil hates it when our response to his assaults is to praise God. Our praise totally frustrates Satan's attempts to defeat or discourage us.

As we endure trials, one of Satan's tactics is to whisper, *"God does not care about you. If He did, He would have answered your prayer by now."* Satan wants us to agree with his lie, rather than God's Word. The truth is that Satan is the one who is blocking the prayer answer. We need to rebuke and resist him.

In my early days of learning spiritual warfare, I once found myself complaining, *"Lord, why have You not performed this promise from Your Word? You promised in Your Word that You would meet all my needs!"* As I was fussing at the Lord, He spoke clearly to my heart, *"Why do you not take that sword you are shaking at Me and shake it at the devil instead!"* Things happen when we start shaking the sword of the Spirit at the devil. *"I rebuke you, Satan. In Jesus' name, I demand that you not hinder God's blessings for me, because His Word promises that He will supply all my needs according to His riches in glory (**Philippians 4:19**). Let go of my finances!"*

The enemy is hindering the release of God's promises, not God! By the Word of God, we need to come against Satan when he tries to block the fulfillment of God's promises.

As a tool, praise accomplishes much. Praise delivers us from fear. Once in a fearful situation, God spoke to my heart, *"Start singing to me, Betty. Sing to me now."* With a trembling voice, I began singing praises to Him. At first, I was shaking all over, barely able to carry a tune, but as I kept praising Him, deliverance came. Within 15 minutes, all fear had left me.

In **Psalm 34:1-4**, note how deliverance from fear follows praise. **"I will bless the Lord at all times ..."** (not merely when we feel like it or when all is going well) **"... his praise shall continually be in my mouth. My soul shall make her boast in the Lord: the humble shall hear thereof, and be glad. O magnify the Lord with me, and let us exalt His name together. I sought the Lord, and He heard me,**

and delivered me from all my fears." Fear cannot stay in the presence of praise. The two cannot dwell side by side. Whenever we begin to praise Him, the fear must depart.

"Bless the Lord, O my soul ..." (Psalm 103:1a). Sometimes our soul does not feel like blessing God, so we have to *command* it to bless Him. Our spirit wants to bless Him at all times. Christ dwelling in us always wants to praise and worship Him. But, when we are not in victory in our soul (which is made up of the mind, will and emotions), we may have to command our soul to line up with what our spirit wants. As we obey and bless God, even when we do not feel like it, our feelings begin to change, and we find ourselves glad to praise Him.

Why should we bless Him? Continuing in **Psalm 103**, we see a few of the innumerable reasons. **"Who forgiveth all thine iniquities; who healeth all thy diseases"** *(not just some, but all)* **"Who redeemeth thy life from destruction; who crowneth thee with lovingkindness and tender mercies; Who satisfieth thy mouth with good things; so that thy youth is renewed like the eagle's. The Lord executeth righteousness and judgment for all that are oppressed ... The Lord is merciful and gracious, slow to anger, and plenteous in mercy" (Psalm 103:3-6, 8).**

God is so good. He has given us so much: salvation, forgiveness, love, joy, peace, healing, blessing, protection and on and on. We have so much to praise and thank Him for. We should never be grumbling and murmuring! Rather, at all times we should be blessing God.

"Rejoice in the Lord always: and again I say, Rejoice" (Philippians 4:4). Our rejoicing, our praise can even bring victory in battle. In the Old Testament, the Israelites defeated some of their enemies through praise alone. In **2**

Chronicles 20, when the Moabites and Ammonites came against Israel, the underdog Israelites sought God for victory. When God's army marched forth, it was led by singers; those appointed to praise God.

"And when he (Jehoshaphat) **had consulted with the people, he appointed singers unto the Lord, and that should praise the beauty of holiness, as they went out before the army, and to say, Praise the Lord; for his mercy endureth forever. And when they began to sing and to praise, the Lord set ambushments against the children of Ammon, Moab and mount Seir, which were come against Judah; and they were smitten"** (2 **Chronicles 20:21-22).** How unusual it is to set the singers at the forefront of an army. But it was God's plan, for when they broke forth into praise, the enemy was defeated! The Israelites did not have to lift a single sword to win that battle.

One reason that praise can bring us victory is that as we praise Him, our spirits are filled with the power of His Holy Spirit. Note the victory that Paul and Silas gained through praise. When they were thrown into prison, they spent their time praying and singing praises. In response, God shook that prison with an earthquake and opened the cell doors **(Acts 16:23-26).** What if Paul and Silas had been murmuring, *"Lord, You have let us down! Here we were out preaching Your Word and You have allowed them to throw us into prison."* If that had been their attitude, they would have missed their release.

Too many of us miss our release because we complain, rather than praise. We may have been serving God, when suddenly the enemy's resistance threw us into some sort of prison. As long as we murmur, and remain upset with God, we will sit in that prison. But once we break forth into praise, our release will speedily come forth. We will walk free from that prison, whether it is one of marital problems or finances or sickness. In fact, regarding sickness, **"A merry heart doeth good like a medicine ..." (Proverbs 17:22a).** It is good medicine for us to sing and praise God no matter what is happening in our lives.

How did John the Baptist handle his imprisonment? Evidently not with praise and faith, for he became filled with doubt, and sent this question to Jesus, **"... Art thou he that should come, or do we look for another?" (Matthew 11:3b).** This was the same John that earlier had declared, **"... Behold the Lamb of God, which taketh away the sin of the world" (John 1:29b).**

We do the same thing. When all is well and we are witnessing the glory of God in our lives, we are certain He is on the throne. But when we start running into problems, we may think, *"Maybe God is not on the throne, after all."*

Note the last portion of Christ's response to John the Baptist's question: **"And blessed is he, whosoever shall not be offended in me" (Matthew 11:6).** Could it be that John became offended with Christ? Maybe he wondered why the Lord was not doing something to release him from prison. Apparently, from the Lord's reply, John became offended with Jesua and began doubting if Jesus really was the Messiah. Yet, John had the key to his freedom, just as we have the key to our freedom. No one can bring us out of our prison unless we agree with God's Word and praise Him in all circumstances. Then God can set us free.

We see an entirely different scene when Paul and Silas were thrown in prison for preaching the gospel. They began praising God and singing when they were put in jail. Praise can bring forth miracles. They were not praising God for being in jail, they were praising God in spite of being in jail because they were serving the living God!

Acts 16:23-26: "And when they had laid many stripes upon them, they cast them into prison, charging the jailor to keep them safely: Who, having received such a charge, thrust them into the inner prison, and made their feet fast in the stocks. And at midnight Paul and Silas prayed, and sang praises unto God: and the prisoners heard them. And suddenly there was a great earthquake, so that the foundations of the prison were shaken: and immediately all the doors were opened, and every one's bands were loosed."

The Tool of Travailing Prayer

Our next tool is the least understood and one that seems like a contradiction to praise. It is the tool of *travail*. Travail is like the pain a mother endures in delivering her child. Spiritually, travail is a type of suffering in Christ or a crying in the spirit. Just as God uses our hands for good deeds and our voices to share the gospel, so He would also use our hearts. He is looking for hearts that will grieve over that which grieves Him. There are things that grieve the Spirit of God; He travails or cries over them. Travail is a godly sorrow. It is not worldly sorrow; there is nothing of self-pity in it.

Many Christians have experienced this travail without being able to identify it. For example, those who have cried out for a burden for souls and then sensed almost a depression may not have realized their hearts were being touched with God's burden for the lost. Those who have wept over souls have been in travail. Often, I have witnessed travail break things that are blocking the answers to our prayers faster than any other tool that we experience. Travail is a powerful tool, one that we can use in spiritual warfare.

Christ travailed. Daniel travailed, crying and weeping before the Lord. Nehemiah was sorrowful before the Lord. Such travail may come upon us as we fast and pray. As we deny our flesh in fasting, we may find ourselves crying over things in the spirit. We may not fully understand this tool, but it accomplishes much in the spiritual realm as we take up deep burdens for others.

"For godly sorrow worketh repentance to salvation not to be repented of: but the sorrow of the world worketh death" (2 Corinthians 7:10). Godly sorrow works repentance. That is why many times God will have us weeping over someone who is in sin. He wants to bring that person to repentance. A worldly sorrow, however, simply works death. Godly sorrow will produce victory. **"They that sow in tears shall reap in joy. He that goeth forth and weepeth, bearing precious seed, shall doubtless come again with rejoicing, bringing his sheaves with him" (Psalm 126:5-6).**

Crying in the spirit is productive; it brings things forth in the spiritual realm. Our travail is not always accompanied by actual crying and tears. It can simply be a heaviness in our hearts and spirits. At times it cannot even be expressed in words; it is beyond utterance. **"Likewise the Spirit also helpeth our infirmities: for we know not what we should pray for as we ought: but the Spirit itself maketh intercession for us with groanings which cannot be uttered. And he that searcheth the hearts knoweth what is the mind of the Spirit, because he maketh intercession for the saints according to the will of God" (Romans 8:26-27).**

The apostle Paul said that he travailed in birth until Christ be formed in the people **(Galatians 4:19)**. Travail brings forth life. It produces spiritual children; sons are brought forth into maturity. **"... as soon as Zion travailed, she brought forth her children" (Isaiah 66:8b).**

Grieving in the spirit can manifest in different ways. Sometimes people may even feel faint or ill. Note Daniel's experience: **"I Daniel was grieved in my spirit in the midst of my body, and the visions of my head troubled me ... And I Daniel fainted, and was sick certain days ... and I was astonished at the vision ... Therefore I was left alone, and saw this great vision, and there remained no strength in me: for my comeliness was turned in me into corruption, and I retained no strength" (Daniel 7:15, 8:27, 10:8).** This feeling of weakness may come during travail. When I occasionally felt faint during prayer, I learned to keep travailing until I prayed the burden through. After that, I always felt fine.

Travail is an effective weapon against the enemy. It is a powerful tool that births things in the spirit realm, produces spiritual children and brings sons into maturity. However, it is also a tool that needs to be used in balance. **"A time to weep, and a time to laugh; a time to mourn, and a time to dance" (Ecclesiastes 3:4).**

The Tool of Fasting

Our final tool is an especially powerful one; that of fasting. It is a tool that is often used when our prayers do not seem to be breaking through. A carpenter knows his handsaw will not go through lumber nearly as fast as his power saw. Adding fasting to regular prayer is like using a power saw; it speeds things up; it hastens the breakthrough. One ministry has called fasting spiritual dynamite. A problem may loom before us like an immovable mountain, fasting will blast it out of our way.

While Biblical fasting involves abstinence from food, it does not mean going without water. There are exceptions to this, such as when Paul went three days without food or water **(Acts 9:9)**. But rarely would a fast without water go beyond three days. Moses had to be supernaturally sustained when he went for 40 days having nothing to eat or drink **(Exodus 34:28)**. The human body can endure a long time without food, but only for a short period without water. After Christ's 40-day fast, He was hungry **(Luke 4:2)**. Nothing is mentioned of thirst, indicating He drank water during His fast.

It is now known that proper fasting actually benefits the physical body. It has a cleansing effect, ridding the body of toxins. So, as we fast, we are reaping both physical and spiritual benefits.

How long should we fast? As long as the Lord leads us to do. A fast could be as short as skipping a meal in order to spend the time in prayer. Remember, it is fasting mixed with prayer that brings results. Denying ourselves food will not accomplish much if we do not also engage in prayer during that time.

Fasting is not an easy tool to use; especially when the enemy tells us that we are unable to go without food. We may even experience a headache or some other physical discomfort, but in Christ we have authority over that. As we deny our flesh and press into prayer and fasting, we will experience spiritual cleansing. Our faith will be built up. We will be able to more readily hear what the Lord would speak to our hearts. We will gain victory over Satan as we loose the bands of wickedness.

Fasting brings our flesh into subjection to our spirit. It is a form of suffering for Christ's sake, and it is ministering unto the Lord.   We should use it as "spiritual dynamite" that is sometimes needed to break through impasses.

God has given us many spiritual tools, and He will show us which tool to use for any given task.   He will reveal to us how we can most effectively battle the enemy, whether it is through a particular type of prayer, through praise and worship, through fasting, or a combination thereof.   Let us use <u>all</u> of these wonderful tools God has given us, that we might walk in the overcoming life, like Christ!

Recognizing the enemy is how we begin our spiritual warfare, but our ultimate victories will rest in obeying our commander-in-chief, Jesus.   He is preparing an army of overcomers whom He plans to use mightily at this time.   By using the tools of spiritual warfare, we can be a part of this mighty army of God.   As we begin winning our individual battles, God will then unite us corporately to win His greater battles in the earth at the closing hours of this age.

ONWARD CHRISTIAN SOLDIERS!

The End

Additional Books by the Authoress, Betty Miller-Haddix

OVERCOMING LIFE SERIES
Book Titles

PROVE ALL THINGS
THE TRUE GOD
THE WILL OF GOD
KEYS TO THE KINGDOM
EXPOSING SATAN'S DEVICES
HEALING OF THE SPIRIT, SOUL & BODY
NEITHER MALE NOR FEMALE
EXTREMES OR BALANCE?
THE PATHWAY INTO THE OVERCOMER'S WALK

END TIMES SERIES
Book Titles

MARK OF GOD OR MARK OF THE BEAST
PERSONAL SPIRITUAL WARFARE

DAILY DEVOTIONAL BOOK
365 Five Minute Devotionals based on the Book of Proverbs

GOD'S WISDOM FOR DAILY LIVING

For digital downloads & printed versions of all books
please visit our website:
https://bibleresources.org/inspirational-bible-books/

Christ Unlimited Ministries
P.O. Box 850
Dewey, AZ 86327, U.S.A.

Post Note

Betty Miller-Haddix serves the Lord as an author, speaker and minister and is wife to Earl Haddix, her new husband; as Bud Miller went to be with the Lord in 2020. As a senior and a widow for a number of years, she continued to write and manage the large website, **BibleResources.org**. This world-wide outreach offers free online Christian literature to the masses. In the fall of 2023, the Lord brought Earl into her life. They have an amazing testimony of how the Lord led them in dreams, and by His anointing, confirming that it was His will that they were to be married. They now continue the work of *Christ Unlimited Ministries* together.

The **BibleResources.org** website offers a Bible search feature, Bible answers, Bible studies, audio Bible readings, "365" daily Bible-based online devotionals, numerous online Bibles, Bible translations, along with the Bible in various languages; plus, many other Bible Resources that have been developed over the last 40 years. Betty and her former husband, Bud, were pioneers in ministry on the Internet. They founded a number of websites in the nineties including **Bible.com**, (which they later sold). Currently Betty and Earl, together, manage **BibleResources.org** and *Christ Unlimited Ministries.*

Betty acknowledges that her anointed gift as a teacher and writer, comes from God. She is a seasoned author of 21 books and a multitude of anointed articles that are posted online on the website and in her Bible Teaching Blog. Betty's most popular and well-known book, that people have read online and in print, is *God's Wisdom for Daily Living.* It is a daily devotional book based on the entire book of Proverbs and is a 365-day, five-minute read. God has anointed and used it to bless millions around the world for years. Since it can be read on cell phones, the Lord is using it to impart the wisdom of the Bible to the world.

Christ Unlimited Ministries, Inc. is a non-profit outreach ministry and is supported by gifts from the body of Christ. Betty and Earl appreciate your prayers, encouragement and support. Your donations and book purchases make it possible for them to share free online teaching literature worldwide, including people in impoverished countries, prisons, and those who otherwise would not be able to obtain them.

Although all literature and books are copyrighted. Many of them have now been digitized and are offered as **free downloads** at the **BibleResources.org** bookstore. Earl contributes his IT talents to help with the online digitized versions of new writings. Betty and Earl offer them to those who are seeking truth and pray the books will bless all who read them. Their desire is for all saints to become great warriors for God!

TO DONATE:
If the Lord speaks to you about helping in this work of God, you can go to:

https://bibleresources.org/church-online/donate/

You can also mail an offering to *Christ Unlimited Ministries*, P.O. Box 850, Dewey, AZ 86327. Checks should be made out to "*Christ Unlimited Ministries*," as this non-profit ministry maintains the **BibleResources.org** website. Thank you in advance.

"The Lord gave the word: great was the company of those that published it" (Psalm 68:11).

For Additional Study

This book is one of two books in the END TIMES SERIES that was taught in Bible School at the Bible Resource Center located in Dewey, Arizona. It is a part of the Overcoming Life Series. The entire series is a virtual "spiritual tool chest," as it covers a multitude of subjects Christians face in their walk with God. It also answers questions that many believers have concerning the current move of God. These are dealt with in a balanced approach and in the light of the Scripture. God's people are not to live frustrated, defeated lives, but rather they are to be victorious overcomers who bring glory to God!

Other Books and Companion Workbooks

PROVE ALL THINGS - (English & Spanish) - Christ warned that great deception would be one of the signs of the end times. In this book, instructions are given on how to recognize false prophets and teachings. Clear Scriptural guidelines are given on discerning the Spirit of truth versus the spirit of error. The book deals with how to judge without being judgmental.

THE TRUE GOD - (English & Spanish) - This is a teaching on the character of God, explaining why God does certain things, and why it is against His nature to do other things. It differentiates between the things for which God is responsible and the things for which the devil is responsible. Our responsibility as Christians, destined to overcome, is made clear so that we can live victorious lives.

THE WILL OF GOD - (English & Spanish) - This lesson teaches us not only how to know the will of God in our personal lives, family, ministry and finances, but also brings understanding as to why God allows sin, sickness and suffering in the world. As overcomers, Christians are not to suffer under many of the things we have accepted as normal.

KEYS TO THE KINGDOM - (English & Spanish) - Instruction on how to gain authority in God's Kingdom through prayer is the topic of this book. Many principles and methods of prayer are covered, such as praying in the Spirit, fasting and prayer, travailing prayer, praise, intercession and spiritual warfare.

EXPOSING SATAN'S DEVICES - (English & Spanish) - This book is a powerful expose' of Satan's tricks, tactics and lies. Cult and occultic methods and groups are listed so Christians can detect their activity. Demon activity and deliverance are discussed. Casting out demons is dealt with in detail. Satan's kingdom is uncovered, and the Christian is taught to overcome through spiritual discernment and warfare.

HEALING OF THE SPIRIT, SOUL AND BODY - (English & Spanish) - This book teaches how to overcome emotional problems, as well as physical ones, and how to receive divine healing. It also teaches how to renew the carnal mind and walk in the spirit of life, thereby overcoming depression, loneliness and fear.

NEITHER MALE NOR FEMALE - (English & Spanish) - What is the woman's role in the church and home? Who is a woman's spiritual head and covering? Does God call women to the five-fold ministry? What does God's Word say about divorce, celibacy and choosing a marriage partner? These and other woman related topics are scripturally examined.

EXTREMES OR BALANCE? - (English & Spanish) - Many Christians have hurt the cause of Christ through "out-of-balance" teachings and demonstrations. This book shows how to avoid those areas. It also deals wisely with the excesses and extremes in the body of Christ.

THE PATHWAY INTO THE OVERCOMER'S WALK - (English & Spanish) - This book contains answers to the questions an overcomer faces as he presses toward the prize of the high calling in Christ Jesus. How can we be conformed to the image of Christ? How does the Holy Spirit work with the overcomers in the end times? What are the overcomer's rewards?

PERSONAL SPIRITUAL WARFARE - Explains the invisible world of spiritual forces that influence our lives and how good can prevail over the evil around us as we prepare for the new kingdom age that is coming. This book will help you overcome problems in your finances, marriage, the emotional pressures of fear, anger and hurt. Here are the keys to victory through spiritual warfare.

MARK OF GOD OR MARK OF THE BEAST - Much has been written and said about the "mark of the beast", but little has been said about the "mark of God". What does 666 mean and what is this mysterious mark? How is it linked to the world of finance? Has this mark already begun? This book answers many questions about the "mark of the beast" and the "mark of God", and how they affect Christians.

GOD'S WISDOM FOR DAILY LIVING - This book is a 365/day devotional based on the entire Book of Proverbs. This unique book is more than just a daily devotional; but is also a series of mini teachings, helping you to both study and meditate on the Word of God. Proverbs reveals the Wisdom of God and helps us know how to deal with the everyday problems that we all face. This book has changed thousands of lives and can change yours as well.

Please visit the web site and click "Bookstore" on the menu for information on how to order or download the complete "Overcoming Life Bible Study." Our site is also an excellent source for additional books and Bible resources.

Contact us at:

www.BibleResources.org
BibleResources@ChristUnlimited.com

Purpose and Vision

Matthew 28:19-20
"Go ye therefore, and teach all nations, baptizing them in the name of the Father, and of the Son, and of the Holy Ghost: Teaching them to observe all things whatsoever I have commanded you: and, lo, I am with you alway, even unto the end of the world. Amen."

Christ Unlimited is not affiliated with any denomination or organized religious group. We are cyber-space missionaries, spreading the good news of Jesus Christ and the empowering truths of God's Word. We also believe we have been called to help establish the Kingdom of God on earth.

Christ Unlimited reaches out to all Bible-believing Christians and non-believers, regardless of their church or denominational affiliations. We are committed to helping wherever possible with evangelistic and teaching outreaches.

Christ Unlimited believes that time is running out and the Gospel has not been preached to every creature. Many nations have not heard the full Gospel, and in many places, doors for evangelism are closing. We believe it is time all Christians cooperated with the Lord in breaking down denominational walls for a united front by His leadership with a frontline advancement against the kingdom of darkness for the purpose of setting up the Kingdom of the Lord Jesus Christ by the power of the Holy Spirit.

Christ Unlimited offers tools to enable the saints of God to help establish the Kingdom of God on the earth. We encourage groups of prayer warriors who will pray, fast, and intercede for the nations. This, we believe, is weapon number one. We teach believers how to overcome through spiritual warfare and through knowing how to use their authority in Christ Jesus by using the Word of God and the power of Holy Spirit.

Christians need to know how to bring down the forces of darkness in their own lives and in the lives of those to whom they minister. We provide, online, such tools as Bibles, teaching literature, Christ Unlimited books and articles directed towards helping people learn how to pray the Word of God. We share the Gospel of Christ (the good news) going forth, by using the Internet to communicate that message. We have teaching materials and Bible school literature focused on winning souls to Christ and building the Body of Christ into maturity. Some local churches and fellowship groups are using the "Overcoming Life Series" study books and workbooks as guides in teaching Biblical truths and the pathway to an overcoming life. Contact us for assistance in setting up a Bible study group or Bible school in your area.

Betty Miller-Haddix serves the Lord as founder of the multi-visioned ministry outreach, Christ Unlimited Ministries. She, along with her husband, Earl Haddix, are called to serve the Lord through maintaining the outreach of the **BibleResources.org** website. The outreach of this ministry has stemmed from a strong desire to see the Word of God taught in its balanced entirety. Betty is a firm believer in prayer, and through prayer, has seen many released from the bondages of fear, failure, and defeat.

The outreach of Christ Unlimited is in obedience to the words of our Lord in **Mark 16:15b: "... Go ye into all the world and preach the gospel to every creature."** This mandate from the Lord presents a challenge to our generation, as many of the world's population still has not heard the Good News of Jesus Christ. Christ Unlimited Ministries also is dedicated to teaching God's Word. **Hosea 4:6a** says: **"My people are destroyed for lack of knowledge ..."**

Many Christians are leading defeated lives simply because they do not know and understand God's Word in a fuller way. Christ Unlimited Ministries is providing for those who desire to know God's Word in a greater way. The main thrust of the teaching and literature is directed at *"How to be an overcomer."* In the end times, we must be prepared to overcome the onslaughts of Satan. Many Christians are suffering needlessly, because they do not know how to overcome sickness, depression, divorce, fear, and financial failure. Christ Unlimited Ministries provides answers for troubled saints and the good news of the gospel to the lost.

www.BibleResources.org
BibleResources@ChristUnlimited.com